Solution

Solution Focused Therapy
A handbook for health care professionals

Dave Hawkes RMN, Diploma Community
Psychiatric Nursing – Certificate in Systemic Therapy

Trevor I. Marsh BA, DipASS, CQSW

Ron Wilgosh RMN, Post Graduate Dip Counselling

OXFORD BOSTON JOHANNESBURG MELBOURNE NEW DELHI SINGAPORE

Butterworth-Heinemann
Linacre House, Jordan Hill, Oxford OX2 8DP
225 Wildwood Avenue, Woburn, MA 01801-2041
A division of Reed Educational and Professional Publishing Ltd

A member of the Reed Elsevier plc group

First published 1998

British Library Cataloguing in Publication Data
A catalogue record for this book is available from the British Library

Library of Congress Cataloguing in Publication Data
A catalogue record for this book is available from the Library of Congress

ISBN 0 7506 1978 3

Typeset by BC Typesetting, Bristol BS31 1NZ
Printed and bound in Great Britain by
Biddles Ltd, Guildford and King's Lynn

Contents

Foreword

I have often said to therapists that I have helped to train – in response to a question or questions – that, once they have an answer then 'you'll have to write that up yourselves'. I am still waiting for many of them to follow through on that task assignment. I must, truthfully, say that when I said this to Dave Hawkes, Ian Marsh, and Ron Wilgosh, I did not even start waiting. I could never have predicted that this motley crew would develop into authors. Good therapists, good trainers, yes, but authors? Thus it was a very pleasant surprise to receive, one day in late 1997, a manuscript. I never would have . . .

As I read through this book, I was struck over and over by their work as illustrated by the transcripts. As I see it, transcripts are the only way that we can really study what it is that clients and therapists do together that is useful. Certainly observing sessions through a see-through-mirror is useful and interesting, but it all happens so fast that most of what is going on is a blur. Videotapes are better since you can employ the rewind button and thus look at a section over and over if you so wish. The transcript is on a printed page and the printed page is something we are very accustomed to studying. We all learned how, more or less, back in our earliest days at school. Indeed, it takes some studying to figure out exactly the connections between what the therapist says and what the client says. This is good for us as readers because once we see those connections, then further linking the interviews with the thinking involved will be easier.

Of course your first impression – prior to studying the transcripts – will have been that Solution-Focused Brief Therapy is very simple. Indeed, perhaps even too simple. But, once you have studied the transcripts, you will find that although the model is simple, it is not easy.

In fact, therapists who work this way will tell you that it takes a lot of self-discipline.

As I read, I was glad to see that Dave, Ian, and Ron included a variety of case examples that cover a wide range of problems often considered difficult. Solution-Focused Brief Therapy is not just for the (so-called) easy cases. In fact, the (so-called) difficult cases are the ones that we can learn the most from. But it doesn't matter. Doing effective therapy depends on finding out what it is exactly that the client wants from the therapy. Once that is clear, then things follow logically.

(I do have one quibble. I disagree with the authors on the use of the term 'Brief' in Solution-Focused Brief Therapy. I think it is essential. From my point of view, Solution-Focused Brief Therapy is brief because it was designed (by me and others) to be brief. 'Brief' is used to mark a distinction between 'brief' and other forms of therapy, for example, 'long-term' therapy, 'family therapy', etc., and I happen to think this is a useful distinction. Of course there are probably as many definitions of the term 'brief therapy' as there are therapists who call their work 'brief'. But my definition, *as few sessions as possible and not one more than necessary*, reminds me of the ethical demand for making any intervention as unintrusive as possible. It is, of course, their choice. (I do not much like the term 'therapy' but I have not been able to figure out what term to use as a replacement.) Furthermore, as I see it, Solution-Focused Brief Therapy is part of a tradition of brief therapy and not a part of other traditions. I think it makes things clear and so I would be sad to see it disappear.)

This quibble, of course, does not detract anything whatsoever from their work or their presentation of their work which I think is very worthwhile and quite well-done. As a handbook, I think it is a good place to start.

Steve de Shazer
Milwaukee

Acknowledgements

Our acknowledgement and deepest thanks go to Steve de Shazer, Insoo Kim Berg, Larry Hopwood, Scott Miller, Ron Kral, Yvonne Dolan and Eve Lipchik for their pioneering spirit, supervision and willingness to share their ideas and time with three over-enthusiastic Englishmen. Steve de Shazer's comment to one of our questions 'you'll have to write that up yourselves' is responsible for this book.

We would also like to acknowledge our clients for their courage with their difficulties and creativity with their solutions.

We are indebted to our colleagues who have worked with us over the past five years as part of our Solution Focused observing teams at the Duchess of Kent Day Hospital, Gloria Gilbey, Gael Odulate, Norman Macdonald, Mary Neal and Sue Frances for their contribution to these ideas.

Thanks also goes to Dr A.J. Macdonald for his information on recent research and WEB sites. Susan Devlin of Butterworth-Heinemann for infinite patience and of course, Julia, Jake, Fraser, Greg, Jean and Sharon for various miracles!

1

Introduction

Things are frequently what they seem,
And this is wisdom's crown:
Only the game fish swims upstream,
But the sensible fish swims down.

When You Say That, Smile by Ogden Nash, 1983

How much dust settles
On the nervous tissue of a life?
Dust has neither weight nor sound,
Color nor aim: it veils, erases,
Obliterates, hides and paralyzes.
It doesn't kill. It extinguishes.
Isn't dead but sleeps...

But it also harbors various seeds,
Half-drowsy ones that will grow into ideas,
Each one close-packed with an unforeseen
Universe, new, lovely and strange.

Dust by Primo Levi, 29th September 1984

Solution Focused Therapy is a model of counselling for individuals, couples and families. While this book is concerned with the practical skills of the approach, the ideas in this book will test your ability to imagine a therapeutic world in which there is no necessary logical connection between a malady and a remedy, other than the presence of one determining the absence of the other.

In some ways this is more of a challenge for established therapists with extensive training, if solutions appear outside the realms of your previous beliefs about the world, this can be an emotionally as well as an intellectually disruptive experience.

On the liberating side, however, it can be very freeing, abandoning hidebound thinking and procedure; working in tandem with the client(s); building solutions and ideas together which can be painlessly discarded if they are not productive.

Similarly, who you see and on what basis can become a liberatingly logical rather than a theoretical endeavour. Previously models of therapy were either 'Individual' in which case one included anyone else at one's supposed peril, or 'Family' in which case one was encouraged to include as many people as possible regardless of whether they thought their presence was either useful or relevant. (This despite the fact that few problems break down under the strict boundaries of being either 'individual' or 'interactional'.)

In Solution Focused Therapy one's behaviour is dictated by the sentiments of the individuals, and the logic of the situation: 'Is there some difficulty which might be helped if 'X' came and we talked. . . . Would they come and how do you think it might help?'. In this way finding solutions becomes a matter of consent, logic and discovery with the possibility of resolving things quickly and without recourse to any theoretical considerations.

One of the tensions of the book is that although the model is an infinitely flexible one, we teach it in a very systematized way, so that someone unacquainted with the model can pull out individual questions or techniques with ease or alternatively work through the techniques 'by rote'. The purpose of this is that the student can become familiar enough with the model to begin to adapt it to the situations in which they find themselves, so that they are able to choose and adapt questions and techniques. Tools such as the scaling questions covered later open up numerous eventualities for the client, both building in the idea of movement, and giving the professional a disarmingly easy way of keeping in touch with how the client thinks the therapy is going.

Our own experience of 'starting off' in the helping professions and going into the professional bookshops was of feeling quite overwhelmed by the amount of knowledge and information that was on display, as if knowledge in itself was power. Years of experience have taught us to cherish the alliance between the client and the therapist, because if this breaks down no therapy is possible, and the techniques here are designed to nurture this working alliance.

So, although as a team we have worked together for ten years in mental health nursing and social work settings, this book does not intend to 'elevate you to the higher levels of theory'. It is designed to teach you some practical and effective questions that can be used with your clients from the first session to the last.

Over time, we learned that no model was sufficient to meet the diverse needs of our client group and found ourselves borrowing techniques from different schools. Clients appeared to find certain things useful, regardless of the approach. These seemed to be founded upon an open and equal relationship with the therapist, a chance to talk about what was most important to them, the opportunity to determine how they wanted to use therapy, and a clear focus for the sessions with the therapist feeding back to the client and being relatively active.

Although these core values are present to some extent in all models of therapy we became aware that certain approaches also put us directly or indirectly in a position of responsibility for the client's problem and its solution.

This has the effect of creating an unbalanced relationship, with the client becoming more passive. In order to live up to this we found ourselves having more and more heated and complex discussions with our peers about what would be helpful. Disappointingly we found this often produced solutions that were so foreign to the client's way of thinking that we damaged much of the useful rapport we had with them in the first place. The more we tried to live up to ideas of being 'expert' the more ineffectual we became. Our desperation seemed to be driving us to become more interested in theories and less interested in people.

Like many professionals at some stage in their development, we were uncomfortable with the way we were working but at the same time were not sure what to replace it with. At this time we became aware of the literature on 'Solution Focused Brief Therapy' and subsequently attended the inaugural workshop by Steve de Shazer (the model's originator) in the UK.

The video case presentations he used were exciting and dramatic examples of clients that we would have previously found difficult to work with changing quite strikingly by the therapist helping the client to utilize their own resources in keeping with this approach. We were so struck by these presentations that we began adopting some of these techniques with our own client group.

The biggest hurdles we had to overcome were learning to believe our clients when they said, 'This is my problem', and to trust them when they said, 'Things have improved'. Our clients taught us that there are possibilities of change in situations where previously we saw none. It may be worth mentioning that our client group includes clients who are diagnosed as 'psychotic', 'depressed', 'anorexic', 'alcoholic' or 'obsessive' and those considered to have been suicidal, survivors of abuse, in relationship difficulties, experiencing anxiety, and work-related stress.

The responses were so encouraging we went, as a team, to Milwaukee, USA, to learn more about this approach by working with de Shazer, Insoo Kim Berg, Larry Hopwood and Scott Miller, taking up residency at the Brief Family Therapy Centre.

Our experiences in developing this approach are contained in the following chapters. The reader should note that one of our earliest experiences, while teaching this approach to other therapists, was that the word 'Brief' in Solution Focused Brief Therapy would often set up an expectation in the therapist that cases should resolve rapidly and that when they found themselves in session 12, 17 or 24 with a client, they would assume that they must be doing something wrong. Clients will resolve their difficulties in their own time, some will take longer than others. We feel the approach is 'brief by outcome' rather than design and in order to avoid the word getting in the way of the therapist–client relationship we as a team no longer use it. The 'Brief' is silent and we as a team talk of Solution Focused Therapy.

In the book you will find a systematized series of techniques that are easily learnt. They are all 'non-toxic' and can be used without harm. Although they will initially seem somewhat cumbersome, familiarity will make the interview far more natural and 'conversational' and give you an easily accessible 'map' of where you are. Similarly, daunting ideas, such as designing interventions, we will try to make simple and accessible even for the newcomer.

The terms 'client' and 'therapist' are used in this book. Wherever 'He' appears we, of course, mean he or she and the word 'therapist' could be replaced by 'counsellor', 'doctor', 'health visitor', 'probation officer', 'policeman', etc., and apply to anyone who finds themselves in a helping conversation.

We have included learning outcomes for relevant chapters and, where appropriate, there are questions to promote further thought at the end of the main body of text. We, ourselves, would have enjoyed such a resource when we started.

We hope you will find this book useful and usable.

2

How to begin: The concepts of Solution Focused Therapy

Learning objectives

This chapter introduces Solution Focused ideas to the reader and provides an outline of a first session of Solution Focused Therapy. Leading contributors to the field are introduced. By the end of the chapter readers will be familiar with the basic assumptions behind the model and tools such as 'the Miracle Question' that help focus on solutions rather than problems.

To practice Solution Focused Therapy you have to begin to think in a Solution Focused way. Some of these ideas may sound strange to practitioners who are used to thinking in a more traditional/theoretical framework. Practitioners such as Eve Lipchik, Bill O'Hanlon and Steve de Shazer have presented these basic ideas in their own distinctive styles. What follows is an overview of Solution Focused ideas.

How it began

Solution Focused Brief Therapy was first developed in Milwaukee, USA, in the early 1980s at the Brief Family Therapy Centre. Steve de Shazer and Insoo Kim Berg put together a team that was interested in cooperation with a client's goals and, in 'exceptions', times when the problem didn't occur. They began to look at what worked in therapy.

They published on these topics in papers such as Brief Therapy: Solution Development (de Shazer et al., 1987), The Death of Resistance (de Shazer, 1984). De Shazer published the model in the books

Keys to Solution in Brief Therapy (1985) and *Clues: Investigating Solutions in Brief Therapy* (1988). Over the next decade or so, a network of professionals have, collectively, developed solution focused ideas. Bill O'Hanlon, Michelle Weiner Davis, Ron Kral, Eve Lipchik, Yvonne Dolan, Ben Furman, Tapani Ahola, Larry Hopwood and Scott D. Miller, to name a few. The authors passed through the Brief Family Therapy Centre in 1992, undertaking their Residency Programme and training with de Shazer, Berg, Hopwood and Miller as supervisors and tutors and so, hopefully, to some extent, the ideas of the Milwaukee teams of the past pass through this book.

Concepts of the approach

Looking for strengths

Solution Therapy believes that clients have strengths and abilities, resources and skills that they bring with them, although they may not be in touch with these parts themselves. They also have made attempts to solve their problems, some more successful than others, but may not give themselves credit for this work due to the overwhelming nature of the distress that causes them to seek help. Solution Therapy attempts to reconnect the client to their own abilities and get interested in their attempted solutions as well as their future potential.

Future orientation

You don't need to know where you are coming from to know where you are going. You just need a good map!

Solution Therapists believe it is useful to build a picture of the client's potential future, how they would like their lives to be. It is not necessary to have an understanding of the past to be able to develop a possibility of the future. Therapists will be familiar with clients who have a well-articulated view of their past which doesn't, necessarily, seem to have helped them. Solution Focused Therapy is about opening up possibilities in future feeling, behaviour and relationships, rather than travelling down what may be historical cul-de-sacs. It would be a mistake to view the world through rose coloured glasses and, as de Shazer states, 'just because we're Solution Focused doesn't make us problem phobic' (1992 quote from discussion with the authors at the residency training programme, Milwaukee, USA).

In fact, Solution Therapists listen to whatever clients feel is important to them but will avoid introducing questions and formulations that add to the area of difficulty, 'tell me more about your difficulties with your mother', in favour of questions such as, 'how would you have liked to be different?'. The latter opens up the possibilities of change and invites a description of a desired scenario without apportioning blame. A common misconception of our approach is that it is restrictive; that we wouldn't wish clients to talk about their past. The approach is, in fact, client led. Nothing is thrown out but we listen to client's histories in a different way, focusing more on what people have learned, need to leave behind, how they would have liked to have been and what difference that would have made to them now. We also focus on their strength in 'surviving' past trauma and stay oriented on how this conversation is proving to be useful. In effect, checking with the client; 'How is this conversation helping?' and 'How will we know we have talked enough?'.

Views on resistant or difficult clients

'Resistance' is a pejorative label that is often assigned to clients by therapists (particularly when the client is not providing the therapist with the answers his/her therapeutic map or training suggests are 'really' necessary).

Solution Therapy sees resistance as a function of the relationship rather than as a personality trait of the client. Resistance is often experienced when the client's goal is different to the therapist. For instance, if a mother wants her son to attend school and the therapist explores the relationship with her husband resistance may be created as the client may not think such discussion is appropriate or relevant. The therapist has, somehow, lost sight of the goal of what the client thinks will help. Such a mother may begin to orient the therapist back to the important issue by repeating herself, changing the subject, asking the therapist to 'consider Jimmy' as he is the reason she attended and may end up asking to see proof of qualifications, to see another therapist or may become irritated and start shouting.

All of these are indications that the therapist is no longer tuned into the client's goal but is instead concentrating on their own. What is more, they can be transformed by the therapist into some idea that the mother is resistant or has a desire to stay the same (traditionally known as 'homeostasis'). Resistance therefore is seen as a function of the difference between the client's world view and the theoretician's frame, rather than a function of the state of mind of the client.

We had long been puzzled by the notion of 'resistance' in therapy. As we watched each other work, we became more and more convinced that clients really do want to change. Certainly some of them found that our ideas about how to change did not fit very well.

Rather than seeing this as 'Resistance', however, we viewed it more as the client's way of letting us know how to help them.

(de Shazer *et al.*, 1986, p. 209)

The occurrence of relationship conflicts is minimized by the solution focused method of working. The Solution Focused Therapist deals with such a situation if it occurs by assuming they are in error and trying to re-focus on what the client wants, e.g., by asking questions such as 'how can we help' or by apologizing and asking the client, 'What would you need to get sorted out today for you to feel this session had been a success?'. Conflicts can then become cooperation. 'If a family does not change, it may be due to the therapist's misunderstanding them' (de Shazer, 1991; Conversation with the authors).

View of change

Change is inevitable. Caring professionals' training often focuses on how hard change is to achieve. In fact, a client returning to a session one week later cannot be *exactly the same*. They have a week's more experience of the world, of the difficulty and of attempted solutions to it if nothing else. Taoists state that stability is an illusion created by the memory of an incident. In fact, people can and will change and we cannot know if such change will be difficult or not *for them*. To apply diagnostic labels or assumptions that a particular problem is more difficult than another is to lose sight of the person or an individual. A Solution Therapist will believe that the client genuinely wants *something* to change, even if this something is someone else. This belief instils a form of genuine therapeutic optimism into the session which can also transmit itself to the client (Irvin D. Yallom, 1931). This belief that people desire change and can achieve it helps the therapist to be seen as genuinely 'in the client's corner'.

Solution Therapy enters the frame of everyday logic if change hasn't occurred. By changing 'psychological theory' to 'issues of logic' Solution Therapy makes sessions more accessible to clients and genuinely conversational. But more of this later.

Simplify

Steve de Shazer uses the maxim, 'Complex problems do not always need complex solutions'. Solution Therapists don't believe there is a necessary correlation between the thickness of the case notes and the difficulty of the case. Therapists habitually rank clients according to a mythological diagnostic league table. In our experience this table has psychotherapy, schizophrenia and personality disorder at one end, and neurotic anxiety and transitional situation disorders at the other. It is presumptuous to believe any problem is difficult to solve until the client has described his ideas about it and what he thinks possible solutions may be. We will suspend such assumptions about difficulty in favour of simply developing a picture with the client of how they want things to be. Also we will accept clients' solutions to problems (provided they are ethical, legal and not dangerous) even if they seem bizarre or unconnected to us. Simple solutions such as walking more, talking more and smiling may in fact help to change complex difficulties.

The client as expert

The client is the expert in their own difficulty. At the European Brief Therapy Conference, London, 1995, we were impressed by the overall theme that emerged about 'staying dumb enough' to ask the client, 'How can I really help?'. Counselling, psychotherapy, psychology, nursing, social work, probation, etc., are often practices that are dominated by theory and technique. Intellectual achievement and the grasping of complex sets of ideas and qualification in theory is held in high esteem. The assumption in our culture is that the therapist qualifies and 'knows'. In fact, Bill O'Hanlon cites a research project undertaken in America in the 1950s (Bill O'Hanlon quote from his workshop 'Solution Oriented Brief Therapy', Edward Lewis Lecture Theatre, London, 11–15 November 1991) where psychology students embarking on a three-year course were tested for basic 'helping skills'. These included appropriate eye contact, non-verbal communication and empathic statements. At the beginning of the course they scored *higher* than at the end, when they apparently had been trained out of these skills in the interest of technique. We try to remember that the idea of 'successful technique', e.g., as described in a case study or video, is often based on the therapist's interpretation of the elegance and fit of a therapeutic process with his theoretical learning rather than through any cross reference with what the client thought was actually helpful. In Solution Focused Therapy, we start from the position that, as Insoo Kim Berg put in conversation, 'we may be able to help in the development of solutions, but the client is the expert in the problem'. We will take up a position of curiosity, of 'not knowing yet' and this allows the client to expand and value their own ideas. This curious, not-knowing position, enhances self-esteem and values the client as well as making therapy a true partnership. This idea of the client as expert reaches its own conclusion in Solution Focused Therapy but has been espoused as a keystone in 'good therapy' in other approaches: 'I think I interpret mainly to let the patients know the limits of my understanding. The principle is that it is the patient and only the patient who has all the answers.' (Winnicott, 1971, p. 84); 'Discard your memory, discard the future tense of your desire, forget them both, both what you knew or what you want, to leave space for a new idea.' (Bion, 1980, p. 11)

Not hypothesizing

The usual procedure in therapy is for the practitioner to look in depth at the referral letter and case notes and draw conclusions about the client. In teams they may ask colleagues for a summary of 'why now' and 'why this symptom'. These are problem focused activities but also constitute the act of 'hypothesize'. Solution Focused Therapists will not hypothesize about a difficulty. In fact, we are flexible and respectful enough to let the clients hypothesize about themselves. Hypothesizing, when it is the act of a team or practitioner generating ideas about a client and then checking them out, restricts the therapist's ability to think freely and so limits his potential to listen to the client in a neutral and curious way. Hypothesizing prior to a session is an activity that excludes the client. There is little chance then for the client to comment on the therapist's thoughts and private agenda and as such it is a disrespectful activity. As Bill O'Hanlon states, 'Every therapist's office should have a couch in it . . . not for the client but for the therapist. When he feels a hypothesis coming on he should lay down on the couch until it goes away!' (Bill O'Hanlon quote from his workshop 'Solution Oriented Brief Therapy', Edward Lewis Lecture Theatre, London, 11–15 November 1991). We believe that suspending the act of hypothesizing until the client(s) arrive and then asking them allows their life events to be co-constructed together. Families will often give their ideas of why, when and where to the therapist and can pick up from the therapist any agenda he has developed. Thoughts can become concrete and thus we see 'hostility' and 'resistance' are phenomena constructed in the therapy setting when the family responds adversely to a therapist-initiated pre-supposition about them. Therapy is more likely to be successful when the client and therapist start at the same place and discover solutions and explanations together, with the therapist honestly and genuinely following the client's lead, rather than engaging in therapeutic pyrotechnics and creating a thousand and one 'needs' for them.

Initially, the therapist does not assume that there is a problem, instead he suspends beliefs about this until the client has the opportunity to explain how he sees the situation. This stance allows the client to present the problem in his own way, and the therapist to listen without prejudice. There is a possibility that the client has not got a problem, for instance that they may have been sent by another family member or professional to solve an issue that they may not see as important. In this case, the motivation to change may not be with the client but with the rest of the family or the GP. Equally, difficulties may have been resolved by the client prior to the appointment. Those more used to a problem frame may search immediately for a difficulty assuming that the reason for the referral must be 'hidden'. If you think along solution focused lines, however, unless there is an obvious reason that suggests otherwise, you are prepared to accept that problems can be solved without you or the client necessarily knowing why and without therapists being involved.

Who should attend?

Solution Therapy is flexible about attendance. We will see anyone who thinks they have a problem (even if that problem is someone else, e.g., their husband). Family therapy has used differing techniques to cope with clients' 'reluctance' to attend. Structural Therapists (such as Minuchin, Fischman, etc.) stated clearly that it was vital the whole family attended whenever possible and may cancel sessions if this could not occur. Strategic Therapists would sometimes 'paradox' members who did not attend by instructing those present to thank them for not coming (since it allowed the family to discuss things that would have been impossible in their presence) and swore the family to secrecy. Systemic Therapists would widen the system to have as many different meanings and ideas about the problem as possible and would see friends, etc., as an important part of the system.

Solution Therapists simply invite clients to 'bring along anyone you feel may be helpful to you in discussing things' and will see one person or the whole family. By insisting on family members being present therapy has at times intimated an hypothesis that the family has the problem of who is to 'blame'. This can lead to defensiveness, even if the desired family member does attend. Solution Therapists aim to minimize blame in what is already a difficult situation, coming for therapy. Solution Therapy can therefore be one-to-one, group, or family-oriented but the choice is with the client and typically you will get the most motivated members of any system who will come along.

How brief is brief?

Solution Focused Therapy is brief by outcome, not by design. De Shazer, when initially expounding the model, chose to acknowledge a debt to the Mental Research Institute (MRI) at Paolo Alto in that he incorporated the word 'brief' in his particular approach. Watzlawick, Weakland and Fisch (1974) designed a specific approach that focused on the problem and how it was maintained and gave the client a 'bank' of ten sessions with which to work on the issues involved. If a satisfactory outcome was reached prior to the tenth session the client had the remaining sessions 'in the bank' for later use with the team. Otherwise they were discharged after session number ten. This was an attempt both to reflect the MRI team's belief in 'induction' (that after ten sessions a therapist was too involved or 'inducted' to keep a perspective on the client's problem anyway) and also circumvent the issue in longer-term therapy that clients really begin to work when the termination of treatment is in sight.

We believe that Solution Focused Therapy controls the sense of 'induction' and 'drift' because the questions themselves provide both a focus and an appropriate therapeutic stance. The aim is always to succeed in as few sessions as possible, to make a small change and get out of the client's way. However, if progress is being made even over a longer period, therapists need not be ashamed or self-conscious about the length of the therapy. We don't believe (unlike other practitioners) that Solution Therapy is a religion. De Shazer said to us in conversation, 'never do anything always'; if you do you are disrespecting the client's individuality. Nobody wants to be analysed to death, behaviourized to death or even 'solutioned to unconsciousness'. Practitioners who focus on the need to be brief rather than be solution oriented, can use the questioning techniques to avoid 'thinking'. It can then become an alienating and impersonal process which has little regard for the client's feelings. We believe it doesn't have to be this way. Once the basic assumptions and way of thinking are mastered, the technique becomes less important than the relationship with the client. Minuchin and Bion championed the cause of viewing therapeutic technique as something to be learned, forgotten and then used instinctively rather than mechanically. Salvador Minuchin, the Structural Therapist (Minuchin, 1974), described the process of becoming a Samurai. Each warrior was sent away without a weapon for a period to learn music, dance, philosophy or anything except the techniques of warfare. They could then return and help the techniques work for them rather than be slaves to mechanics. Guntripp, in sessions with Winnicott (the famous child psychotherapist), describes how the ideas arose naturally out of conversation. Remember that is all therapy is . . . conversation.

Some problems take longer than others and clients also move at their own pace. One of the advantages of this approach is that even the most difficult cases can be seen less intensively than traditional models recommend (in our experience very few clients ask to be seen weekly, and 18 sessions over 24 months is still a cost-effective method of both therapy and support).

One of the most important issues about Solution Focused Therapy is that it attempts to take the most efficient and direct way towards a solution. All of us have areas of choice in our lives, an ability to think and to make decisions. Rather than assuming that the fabric of our lives is tied to an underlying sub-structure of roots and difficulties, Solution Focused Therapy believes that movement may actually be facilitated by 'disregarding' such assumptions.

Science in the twentieth century and 'therapy' (a much younger cousin of science) has attempted to comfort us with the belief that we can predict the actions of nature and promotes the idea that there is a clear connection between cause and effect. (For example, our adult personalities are determined to some extent by trauma, parental habit, behavioural patterns or biology.) This leads us to believe that our actions are pre-determined and limited in a way that is not healthy for us or our imaginations, and that we can only solve these problems in particular ways according to particular rules. Shakespeare may have been right when he wrote in Hamlet, 'There are more things in heaven and earth Horatio than are dreamt of in your philosophy' (Shakespeare, 1991). There is always a fresh path to take, an 'exception'.

Chaos theory has emphasized that many seemingly simple processes have quite unpredictable results. The world is both open to influence and unpredictable (see Vincenzi, 1994). Therapists should not try and undermine this but 'go with the flow'.

One of the advantages of practising Solution Focused Therapy (even for the hardened theorist) is that over any period of time there will be a number of cases whose outcome will be absolutely unpredictable in terms of the previous theory they espoused. Given this fact, one is left with qualifying the outcome in some peculiar way quite out of tune with the patient's seeming satisfaction in order to 'save the hypothesis', or simply accepting that both life and therapy are rather more unpredictable.

Simple questions and brief resolutions do not mean that you will not get sophisticated and impressive results. Also, clients introduce refreshing and usable ideas to therapy.

Helping professionals are usually educated in the art of problem solving. This involves assessment of the 'depth' of the problem, its origins, its regularity and its cause and only then moving on to resolving it. To conduct a solution focused first session it is helpful to regard problem solving and solution finding as two unrelated processes. Problem focused questions such as when, where and how do these symptoms occur, act to rectify the problem. The more you talk about it, the harder it is to solve. These principles can be summarized by 'Americanisms' (Berg and Miller, 1992).

If it ain't broke, don't fix it

A Solution Focused interview begins without assuming there *definitely* is a problem. Techniques such as asking 'how can we help?', and the later scaling questions allow clients to tell us if they have already solved the problem. We stay within the client's definition of the problem, e.g., families are not the 'cause' (unless the client says so). Marriages are not the 'trigger' (unless they say so) and even gender and cultural issues would be seen as irrelevant unless they feature in the client's presentation. If we have a 'hunch' it is better to share it and let the clients have the opportunity to confirm or deny our hypothesis. Similarly, we wouldn't assume intrapsychic issues were at work (e.g., repressed material, childhood trauma, a distorted view of the world, etc.) unless the client clearly presented these issues as a focus. Perhaps the hardest element of this approach is trusting clients to be able to bring these issues to therapy and think and make connections (in effect to hypothesize to the therapist about their lives rather than the other way round).

If it works do more of it

If questions, puzzles, homework tasks, certain messages or behavioural changes help the client move closer to their goals rather than search around for something clever or different to say you can keep doing more of the same. A significant amount of time in a first session is consigned to finding out what does work for the client now. This frees the therapist from the need to be an expert or sell a solution to the client. It keeps the relationship equal by giving clients' attempted solutions credit and importance.

If it doesn't work do something different

This statement is what saves Solution Focused Therapy from becoming a 'religion'. Philosophically, Solution Therapy is an open set of interventions and possibilities with a preference for behavioural change and description. It is not a science or technically a theory.

We have found that there is a critical point in most therapeutic thought where contradictions become apparent. For instance, how can Solution Therapy be client led but also not interested in their past experiences, since clients may be preoccupied or disturbed by them? This basic idea allows considerable flexibility. The approach is pragmatic and centred on the question, 'How can I best help this client?'.

The Solution Therapist has got no interest in vindicating a theory (any theory, even his own) but is searching for the best result for the client in the client's own terms. Therefore the therapist is always checking with the client: 'Is this helping?'; 'Is this change enough for you?'; 'What else needs to happen for you to be satisfied with the situation?'; 'What else do we need to talk about?'.

After three sessions or so, if nothing has changed, the therapist will be prepared to thoroughly review the situation: 'Am I helping?'; 'Is the approach helping?'; 'What do you feel would help you move on further?'; 'Is the goal you set in the first session realistic?'; 'Is there something you want to change about your original goal?'; 'Do you really want the life you've described?'; 'Is there anything you hoped I would ask about that, that would really help you?', and will change pace, focus, style or use questions from another approach to move forward. Dvorah Simon (1992) states that, 'It's solution focused to look for solutions, even if they are outside the frame of Solution Therapy'. Therefore, the idea of a therapist not being solution focused enough only makes sense if they've lost touch with the client's goals, since any activity that helps the client move on respectfully, can be considered a solution focused activity.

Summary

To begin you may have to unlearn many of the principles of traditional approaches to mental health. Change becomes inevitable; lasting change can be possible in a few sessions; cause and effect becomes secondary compared to what is going to happen next; the client is an expert on their own difficulties, hypothesizing to the therapist; and the therapist stays focused on their goal and is prepared to cooperate with it (up to the point at which it may become unethical, immoral or dangerous). Even goals such as 'to get out of this ward' are seen as realistic building blocks and the questions become: 'What would happen to get the next step nearer going home?'; and 'What would your family have to see to convince them things were different?'. Developing this common goal is what makes the approach useful with clients who are sent or are legally bound to attend, since the goals are relevant to them making joint work worthwhile for the client. So how do you structure a first session to encompass all of these basic assumptions?

The Milwaukee model: structure of the first session

Solution Therapy, since its inception, continues to grow and develop. The standard session involves a number of activities. These include:

- an invitation to the client to express their perception of the need for therapy, their expectations of therapy and of the therapist
- the establishment of goals that are salient to the client through a detailed description of the desired future scenario
- the exploration of existing successful behaviours, successes and resources that can act as the building blocks for change
- an assessment of the client's motivation to change and their perception of how realistic it is that change can occur
- the sharing of a message that summarizes the session and may include tasks for the client to try.

The therapist believes that the client can and will change and that he has already attempted solutions to the problem (some more useful than others). The interview is conducted to discover what the client is already doing that is good for them and that may provide a solution and what more can be done to ensure continued success.

3

Stages of a first session of Solution Focused Therapy

(items in brackets are optional)

- **What brought you here today?**
  What needs to happen for today to be a success?
- **How can I help?**
  (How will that help?) (optional)

  Listen

- **The Miracle Question**
  'Suppose you go home from here this evening and you go to bed and go to sleep. While you are asleep a miracle happens (and the problem that brought you here to see me today is solved just like that). Because you were asleep you don't know how it happened. Anyway a miracle happens, what would be the first thing you would notice that would tell you something is a little different today, that a miracle must have happened during the night?
  What else?'
- **Relationship questions**
  'What would your wife/husband/boyfriend/partner/boss/mother, etc., see you doing that would tell them?
  What would you notice different about them if this miracle happened?
  If I was a fly on the wall what would I see you doing differently that would tell me things are better?
  Who else would notice that this miracle has happened?

What else would be different?'
Translate absences of symptoms into beginnings of new
behaviours.

- **Exception questions**
  'Are there any times when even small parts of this miracle
  happen now?'
  'What helps even a little?'

- **Scaling questions**
  Where are you now scale
  'On a scale of 0 to 10, where 0 is the worst you have been and
  10 is the day after a miracle, where would you be today?'

  Willingness to do (motivation scale)
  'On a scale of 0 to 10, where 10 is that you would do anything
  to solve this problem and 0 is that you would just like to think
  about it, where would you be today?'

  Confidence scale (optional)
  'On a scale of 0 to 10, where 10 is you are very confident you
  could solve this problem this time and 0 is that you think there
  is no chance you can solve this at the moment, where would
  you be?'

- **Is there anything you wanted to tell me or I missed?**

  Break

- **Message**
  Compliments/validation

  Bridging statement
  'Because you've said . . . , I'd like to suggest . . .'

  Task (infinite)

Our sessions last a maximum of one hour with the therapist taking
the role of time keeper. The length of session varies in relation to the
demands of the institution. Practitioners have considered 20 minute
interviews (conversation with Eve Lipchik) and Ron Kral, who worked
in education, described students calling across the corridor to him,
where they were on various scaling questions in a few seconds; 'I'm on
8 Ron!!', etc. On a busy ward the session may be part of a 10 minute
conversation and the questions can be used in isolation from each
other simply to introduce some therapeutic potential to everyday
client/carer conversations. In our clinic at a psychiatric day hospital

we use a team which provides 'live supervision' from behind a one-way screen while the client sits with the therapist. Clients are aware of the team and will be introduced to them if the clients prefer. They can also ask not to have the screen or any observing professionals. The team may comment by knocking on the door and asking the therapist to ask something if they feel he is missing anything or can comment on the client's strengths or abilities, etc. The team in Solution Therapy is there to help generate questions and interventions tend not to be as active as in other models since solutions are generated by the client and therapist rather than by an 'expert' team. This client choice contrasts with strategic approaches to the screen, where the team is a mysterious entity that the client has no influence over.

It is important for the reader to understand that teams, video links and live supervision are all preferable, but not essential. The authors have used modified first sessions in clients' homes, in offices and in group therapy. They have adopted the approach as an assessment tool for admission wards and day hospitals as well as creating a solution focused model of the nursing process, applicable regardless of clinical setting. It has been used in telephone counselling services (similar to Britain's Samaritans) and our colleague John Flynn (UK) successfully used it with children and adolescents while working for a national abuse helpline. The adaptability of the approach to ward, staff supervision, business, staff appraisal and personnel issues is one of its greatest strengths.

We usually receive a referral letter in our practice and we read the letter but do not generate any hypothesis before meeting the client. Theoretically, some practitioners would say it is not necessary to have any information about the client but we have found reading the information respectful since clients often ask us, 'have you read my notes', and it also respects the referrer, who may be concerned about an issue that the client may not easily share. The following 'map' then applies.

What brought you here?

This question invites the client to describe the events and experiences that have resulted in their attending therapy. In response, the client may talk about a life that currently includes drinking too much, feeling anxious and/or depressed, may mention conflict with their partner, an inability to go out to work, and so on. As professionals trained to recognize, respond to and explore pathology, we could understandably react to any or all of these complaints.

Until the client states what they expect from us we would suspend any assumptions about this material. We do not know at this stage

what help the client is seeking and would not begin any kind of therapeutic activity until the client's expectations of us are clear. We assist
this process of clarifying goals as early as possible by asking 'How can
I help?'.

How can I help?

This question invites the client to take some initial responsibility for
the direction of the therapy and results in their having to think carefully about what specific interventions they think would be helpful
to them. The therapeutic stance immediately established is one of
collaboration, with the client taking the lead rather than a relationship
in which they are passive and wait for 'the expert' to get them 'better'.

'How can I help?' begins to define the therapeutic relationship even
if the client is unable to respond initially; at least it starts people thinking about exactly what they want from the therapeutic relationship. As
the client begins to suggest further ideas we may ask questions such as,
'How will that help?' or 'What difference will that make to you?', so
that we can begin to understand better the steps the client needs to
take to enable them to make progress. A great many of our clients
respond to the question by saying, 'I would just like you to listen'.
They do not, necessarily, ask us to deal with their drinking, anxiety,
depression, voices, marital conflict or work problems.

Even if we are asked just to listen, we may still wish to know 'How
will that help?', hopefully to get a picture of how long the 'listening'
may take, how this will be helpful to the client and what use they will
make of the conversation. For example:

Client: 'I'd like you to listen.'
Therapist: 'How will that help?'
Client: 'Well, I can't talk to anyone in my family and I need
             support to help me decide whether to leave home or not.'

In this example, 'How will that help?' has put the 'listening' firmly
in the context of a goal. Listening becomes an active process, as a
means to an end (decision making) rather than an end in itself (self
exploration).

The other advantage to using these questions is that a certain
number of clients do not come for 'therapy', but merely want information or advice and these questions allow the therapist to realise this
and enter the relationship at the same level as the client, allowing the
client to present a simple problem rather than a complex one.

During the early stage of the session, clients need to feel that the
therapist understands the seriousness of their difficulties. Solution

Therapy, initially, tried to disrupt this 'problem talk' by asking questions about the clients' strengths and abilities or complimenting them on their ability to cope with such problems. This attempt to encourage as much conversation about positives as possible was categorized as a section of the interview titled 'non-problem talk'. The Milwaukee team dropped this because it can easily be seen as 'rose-coloured spectacles', and can result in the client further emphasizing their difficulties because they do not feel that the therapist has understood. If the client is left with the feeling that they have not been heard, they will not be able to move on to fully explore issues about the future. De Shazer states that 'just because we are solution focused, doesn't mean we are problem phobic'.

Instead of 'non-problem talk' the development in theory now suggests that the therapist listens, respectfully, with some level of empathy, but does not elaborate the difficulties by paraphrasing or asking for more detail about the problem. The session can be described as having a 'critical mass' and clients will invite the therapist to comment once they feel they have said all they want to say. These invitations take the form of questions, e.g., 'I don't know, what do you think?', pauses or repetition. The Solution Therapist is receptive to these indications and will initiate the next stage of the session when it is respectful to do so. Not all clients need to talk at length about their problem and the Miracle Question can be asked very early in a session, if appropriate.

We are often asked at training events, 'when do you ask the Miracle Question?', and rules of thumb would include if the client is vague and, after some discussion, there is still not a picture of how you can help, or in couples work, when a routine argument ensues or, when the client runs out of steam.

Introduction to the Miracle Question

De Shazer tells a story of interviewing a client and asking him about what it would take for things to change and of him replying, 'Well it would need a miracle'. This was elaborated by the Milwaukee team into a question which became a fulcrum of their approach. Therapists, de Shazer says, unlike business men, are not interested enough in goals. Without goals therapy can last forever. Without goals how does either the therapist or client know they are on the 'right track'?

Insoo Kim Berg cites Milton Erickson as using this kind of question when he was interviewing clients, usually, when they were in a trance. He would form a 'crystal ball' inside which the client could travel through time to learn things about themselves. Erickson would send clients into their own future to find out how they had, eventually, solved the problem, what they felt like to be free of their difficulty and what steps they had taken to arrive at a solution. He would, also, send the client into the past to find things they would like to keep about themselves and their present symptoms that may help them be stronger in the future.

de Shazer and his team found that clients could explore their future in some detail without being in a formal trance. The Miracle Question (de Shazer, 1988) does keep its impact on clients. It is phrased in such a manner to encourage the clients to dissociate completely from their present difficulties and imagine a world in which there are only good things and achievements. Technically, this question can be seen as a future-oriented hypothetical question. Other less elaborate forms of such a question would be: 'How would you like things to be?'; or 'What will be different when this problem is solved?'.

Culturally, the concept of a miracle does not always sit easily in a European setting and colleagues have fed back to us that it sits even less easily with a Muslim culture. Some practitioners have adopted questions such as: 'If you had three wishes what would be different?'; 'If you had a magic wand what would you have different in your life?' (very good with children); or 'If this was the last episode of a television drama in which everything turned out OK what would be different between you?'.

With clients who find it difficult to think in terms of the Miracle Question, using scales of 0 to 10 (with 10 being the best their life could be) the therapist can explore what 10 would look like, where the client is now, and what they would settle for, as well as what others would be noticing about the client at 10 or what others would be doing differently when they are at 10. Solution therapy has a strong idea of fit and some clients fit better with questions worded in a more concrete fashion.

In most circumstances, if there are no clear, cultural, intellectual or religious difficulties, we prefer to use the Miracle Question in its entirety, usually preceded by an apology for its strangeness, since the unusual nature of the question can be a factor of its success.

The Miracle Question

'I'm going to ask you a strange question. Supposing you go home from here and go to bed and while you are asleep a miracle happens. You don't know it's happened because you are asleep but a miracle has happened and the problem that brought you to see me is solved. When you wake up, what would be the first thing that would tell you something is different today, that a miracle must have happened in the night?'

The aim of the question is to get a detailed description of a future scenario in positive, behavioural terms, i.e. what will be present in the future rather than what has disappeared? Clients often answer with statements such as, 'I wouldn't be arguing with the children'. This is a negative statement and the therapist needs to ask, 'What would be happening instead?' to change the answer into the beginning of something rather than the absence of something. De Shazer contends that it is impossible to think of what *not* sitting on a white chair would be like, without thinking of what the experience of sitting on one *is* like. As the aim of the Miracle Question is to dissociate the patient from his problems, and because it is very difficult to be sure when something has stopped (it may come back), the only true test of whether the problem is ended is whether the patient has fulfilled a 'good enough' description (of the goals he wishes to pursue).

Relationship oriented questions

The therapist then goes on to ask relationship oriented questions such as: 'What would be the first thing that your wife would notice that would tell her that a miracle has happened?'. Relationship questions provide added richness to the miracle picture. They also give further information about what the rest of the family think and what their ideas of a miracle would be: 'What would your mother notice that was different about you?'; 'What would the children notice that was different about you?'. These questions are then cross referenced with the idea of what the client would notice that was different about the family: 'If this miracle happened, what would you notice different about your wife?'; 'If you were doing all this, how would the kids be different towards you?'; 'If the kids were like that, what effect would this have on your wife?'.

These questions empower the client, making him feel important in his social network and explores the effects of change in more depth. They can, also, motivate clients who can then see what the benefits of changing would be. With isolated clients, or those who are preoccupied with their own difficulties, this may be the first time they have been asked to think of others in this way. 'What would people at work notice different about you?'; 'Who else would notice?' or 'What would your psychiatrist/probation officer notice?', are also alternative relationship questions, as are hypothetical scenarios when appropriate: 'If your mother was still with us, what would she say would be different about you?'; 'If I was a fly on the wall in this miracle household, what would I notice different about you?'.

If problem talk re-emerges, e.g., 'We'd be talking more because he doesn't even talk to me', the therapist re-orients to the start of a positive behaviour with a question such as 'After the miracle, how would this be different?'.

Any paraphrasing, non verbal and verbal feedback, positive statements or comments that help the client talk about this miracle can be used by the therapist to get as detailed a picture of new behaviours as possible. It is important that the therapist does not expect textbook answers to these questions. Clients come to therapy, often with a preconception of questions the therapist will ask, and the Miracle Question is unusual to them. Therefore, popular, initial answers are 'I didn't know', or 'I'd win the lottery'. The important thing is not to panic. Clients will think about these issues even if they cannot answer the question in the session. Also, unrealistic goals are quite common at this stage. The aim is to allow people to have their dreams at this stage and, gently, to facilitate smaller steps and realistic outcomes later in the session (with techniques such as exception and scaling questions). From these unrealistic goals can appear small parts of a miracle which can be picked up and cooperated with by the therapist. For example:

CL: 'I'd win the lottery.'
TH: 'How would that help? What would be different?'
CL: 'I'd be able to take a break and travel, go out with my mates and relax more.'

These latter goals may be achievable through other means than the improbable lottery victory. By following this path gently, through unrealistic goals, rather than directly challenging the client (e.g., 'How are you going to do that?') the therapist maintains momentum in the session and allows the client to voice their miracle without judgement. Goals such as 'My husband would still be alive' can be followed through to present realistic steps if the therapist sensitively asks, 'We know this isn't possible, but how would it help?'; clients we have seen have then answered 'I wouldn't feel so awkward about going out with friends who are all couples', 'The finances would be taken care of by someone else for a while', etc. Again, these goals can be cooperated with without encouraging wild or unrealistic fantasies. Of course, it is important in bereavement to let people go through whatever emotions they need to rather than generating alternatives to loss too quickly, but when the client lets you know when they are ready to move on then these questions can be useful in helping them re-cast their lives. Alternative steps to achieve goals such as feeling more confident and going out more can open up options to clients who previously tie themselves to only one impossible solution to a problem.

This attempt to explain discussion about the preferred future scenario is highlighted by Ben Furman (Finnish Therapist) in his book *Solution Talk* (Furman and Ahola, 1992). He expands possibilities and the aim of the therapist's 'what else?' and examines how 'relationship questions' are to develop with the client as many different signs of improvement and parts of a solution as possible. *Solution Talk* suggests many different paths he can begin to take which will lead him towards his goals. Scott Miller (American Solution Therapist and Ericksonian Hypnotherapist) describes this process as 'developing multiple end-points' (discussion with Scott Miller, Milwaukee Residency Training, 1992). Literally, the more solution talk there is in a session the more likely the client is to engage in some activity that is successful between the first and second sessions. Also, logically, if the client has a rich and detailed picture about what he would be doing then this will orient him in terms of his future activity.

Exception questions

The early generations of the Milwaukee team, de Shazer, Insoo Kim Berg, Michelle Weiner Davis, Eve Lipchik and Ron Kral, were all interested in exceptions to a rule. There are always exceptions, times when the problem is not so intense, when the client can cope better, or when there is a better hour in the day. Solution Therapy is curious about these occurrences since the exceptions tell us as much about the client and his difficulties as problems or symptoms do. De Shazer paraphrased the philosopher Wittgenstein during a conversation with the authors by stating that 'the only interesting thing about a problem is that it contains within it some idea of a solution'. In order to state that we are 'depressed', we must have an idea about what not being depressed is like.

After the miracle and relationship questions have defined how the client would like this to be, the therapist asks, 'Are there any small parts of this miracle happening already?'. This question allows the therapist to discover any existing behaviours that help the client, any solutions that they have recently tried and any changes that have occurred prior to the session. De Shazer suggested that a large percentage of clients reported positive changes prior to attending therapy. Such exceptions are useful since all credit can be given back to clients for the steps they have already taken without the therapist's help. English researchers at the Tavistock clinic (Malan, 1968, 1975) found that clients on a waiting list for therapy reported both 'psychodynamic' and 'symptom-based' change in the time between referral and the commencement of therapy. This suggests that the act of seeking help focuses clients on their life and how to change it. Exception questions allow the client to share this information.

Negative responses to exception questions are simply accepted and the therapist proceeds to the next state.

Scaling questions

Scaling questions represent the part of the session where the client begins to break the miracle into smaller, more manageable steps. They provide a useful assessment tool and a sense of movement which would not be given by simple 'either/or' closed questions (e.g., 'Are you depressed?'). They can be used as an alternative to the Miracle Question and incidentally provide information that can be recorded for the purpose of a problem focused document (e.g., risk assessments for suicide or aggressive behaviour or hospital medical assessments). We are often asked by professionals how to document solution talk for the purposes of existing problem focused systems, and scales provide some information that can be commonly useful to Solution and Non-Solution practitioners. The idea of a numerical scale is not essential since with children or adults with learning difficulties marks or lines on a blackboard between two points or pictorial versions of hill or mountain climbing, etc., can be used. Scales can be used for anything, a standard repertoire usually includes:

1. **Where are you now scales**
   'On a scale of 0 to 10, where 0 is the worst things have been and 10 is where you would like your life to be, where are you now on the scale?'. Wording can change as appropriate, e.g., 'Where have you been on the scale in the last week on average?', and split scales can be used, e.g., 'What is the highest you have been over the last week?; What's the lowest you have been?'.
2. **Confidence scales**
   'On a scale of 0 to 10, where 10 would be where you're certain you can change this and 0 is where you don't think you have a hope, how confident are you?'
3. **Motivation**
   'On a scale of 0 to 10, where 10 is that you'll do anything to solve the problem and 0 is that you'll just hope and pray, where are you now?'
4. **Risk assessment**
   'On a scale of 0 to 10, how worried should I be about you hurting yourself, killing yourself, hitting your wife, taking drugs, etc., in the next fortnight?'

These scales provide the therapist with a useful check on where the client is and how hard they are prepared to work in order to change things. The possibility of movement is inherent in asking a scaling question. For instance, if you ask 'Where are you now?', then the answer of '3' allows you to follow up by asking: 'How did you get from 0 to 3?'; What would $3\frac{1}{2}$ look like?'; 'How come you haven't slipped back to 2?'; 'What are you doing that keeps you at 3?'; 'What would your wife be doing at $3\frac{1}{2}$ that she isn't doing now?', etc. Even an answer of '0' can produce the response, 'How do you cope?', which will tap into the client's positive resources and support network. Obviously, the therapist does not persevere until the client reaches their miracle; 'What will you settle for?' can realistically set targets and often 7 or 8 is 'good enough'.

Similarly, answers on the confidence and motivation scale help to orient both the client and the therapist to the assumed degree of diffi- culty the client sees as inherent in the problem. These scales help the therapist to decide on the level of cooperation he can expect from the client and orients him to the kind of intervention that would be appro- priate. For example, a client who is low in confidence and motivation will not be asked to carry out an elaborate homework task. Exploration of these scales at such a basic and concrete level make families (some- times painfully) aware of how the referred person sees the situation and how likely/able he is to do anything about it. The realization, for instance, that an adolescent is 8 on his contentment scale and is 1 on his motivation to get a job may change the construction of the situa- tion in their mind, of whose problem is it anyway and who is likely to do anything about it.

New therapists often find the scales repetitive and the temptation is to drop the confidence scale. However, this scale is important in that it gives us information about whether the change required is within the client's control or not. For example, someone may be 10 on motivation but 1 on confidence since they are certain that they won't have the money, that a house or a job will not be possible or that another person will prevent them from achieving their goal. This then allows the therapist to accept the difficulty as outside of the client's influence and, therefore, the goal as unrealistic. Then it becomes a question of, 'What will the client settle for, or while they are waiting for a job/ money/change of boss, etc., what can they do to make their life a little better?'. This allows the client to have an agenda about housing, poverty, etc., and the therapist to address these, rather than assuming automatically that everything is within the client's control. Sometimes a letter to housing, a call to the GP, reading a letter from a college to discern its meaning, etc., are within our power as clinicians and can have practical benefits for our clients.

Scales can all be relational, e.g., expanded by asking, 'How confident would your wife be of you giving up alcohol this time?', 'What would she need to see to raise this confidence just half a point?'.

Is there anything else?

After asking scaling questions, it is 'good housekeeping' to ask the client, 'Is there anything else you wanted to ask us about, or that we needed to know before we take a break?'. This question allows the client to discuss anything that they still need to discuss or did not feel confident enough to broach earlier in the session. This question broadens the session. Any issues can be further explored with the clients prior to the intervention break. This obviates the possibility that both you and the client will go through the session format without the client bringing something important to the therapy. On occasion, this has been the time that clients have chosen to disclose painful or difficult information that they could not trust us with earlier in the session. Issues about violence and abuse are as important to a Solution Therapist as anyone else. As we discussed, the aim is not to actively steer the session away from anything but to ensure that the focus of work is client led.

The intervention break

At this point in the session, the therapist takes a break. This occurs whether he is working with a team of therapists, is by himself or visiting the client at home. Family Therapists had often used a break in therapy as a 'technique'. It was thought useful to leave the therapy room to discuss issues with the therapy team. There is a certain dramatic effect which can focus the client's attention on the imminent message and heighten its impact. Physically removing yourself from the session helps you to get your thoughts together and develop the intervention. We always take a break even on home visits, although we understand some people will not see this fitting with their practice. Obviously the worker, as well as the client, has got to feel comfortable with these techniques and will adapt them accordingly. The Brief Family Therapy Centre were the first to regularly take a break with or without a team, with or without a mirror (Correspondence with de Shazer, 1998).

Tasks and interventions

The therapist and his team (if he has one) will endeavour to summarize the session, provide the client with a focus for thought or suggestions for action, and support the client in any attempt to solve the problem. The decision about a further appointment is made at this stage, based on the material from the session if it is clear that they would want another appointment. We try to arrange this prior to delivering the intervention so that further discussion (dates, times, etc.) doesn't detract from its impact.

Previously, tasks and interventions were seen to be of crucial importance. In Solution Therapy, the session itself is usually seen as an intervention, and the task grows naturally out of the material. This absolves the therapist of the responsibility of developing something 'eloquent' or 'marvellous', since in this approach it is the clients who make the intervention from their responses to the Miracle Question and scaling questions, and who ultimately make a task successful or unsuccessful.

Interventions can be broken down into three stages:

1. Compliments
2. Bridging statement
3. Task.

Compliments

The first component of an intervention is often the easiest to construct. Therapists look for genuine positive statements to make about the client to amplify and value their attempted solutions and their strengths. These compliments must be genuine and low key (particularly in British culture). Clients do not usually expect to be valued in therapy or to have their strengths explored as well as their weaknesses. Compliments provide a balance for clients who are often overwhelmed by 'failure'. An example of the power of positives is given by a story a colleague told us about Peggy Penn (USA). She was seeing a woman and had developed a complex message for her. She delivered the message with the 'throwaway line', 'You are a very intelligent lady', and went on to deliver what was the 'important' part of the message, exploring family myths that may have contributed to the woman's belief about life and her present difficulties. In the next session the client said how helpful the last message had been. Peggy re-stated the family patterns and how the client had thought about them, only to have the client state, 'I didn't hear any of that. . . . You said I was an intelligent woman and I thought "I am an intelligent woman, I'll show them"'. The compliment had helped the client to make change and Peggy Penn realised then that a client will often take what fits for them from an intervention and can often turn a mediocre message into something quite wonderful.

Compliments should be genuine, developed with that particular client in mind and the choice of which type to use will depend on how the client has reacted during the session. They should never be learned by rote but for the beginner examples are:

'We're impressed because things have been really tough, but still you want to sort things out.'

'Thank you for coming, taking time out of your busy schedule to see us.'

'It's obvious from what you've said that you really love your children.'

'Though you've felt very low, you have been able to keep working and take care of your family and that's impressive.'

'You obviously have a good sense of humour and you say that helps you cope.'

'You've really made a start on this problem.'

'You've clearly battled hard and overcome a lot to get this far.'

'If you didn't care this much for each other, you wouldn't be here and this is clear to us.'

'You've really thought a lot about this problem and how to solve it.'

'You've managed to hold on this long.'

'You've been responsible to your partner, that's good for both of you.'

'How did you know this was the right thing to do?'

'Thank you for being so open and honest today, you've helped us to get an idea about things.'

Compliments can be direct like, 'You're an intelligent person', or 'You've really handled that well', or indirect like, 'Your children have done really well'; or 'You've really sat there and thought about this'.

Some clients do not accept compliments easily and it is important that the therapist doesn't 'wrestle' clients into accepting them. Clients who come back with 'Yes, but' are educating the therapist to either use very gentle indirect compliments or to prefix them with a comment such as 'I know you don't take compliments easily but I feel that you are clearly a good mother', etc.

Bridging statement

This demonstrates to the client that you have heard what he said during the session and appreciated what he hopes to achieve through coming. It explains any task of comment to the client and sets it in a proper context. It takes the form of a statement 'Because you said that you want to . . . we'd like you to . . .'. For example; 'Because you've said that you really want to save this marriage and care for each other, we'd like you to notice what the other person does that makes you feel valued and helps things between you.' The bridging statement is not a complex matter. It is important to make a straightforward link between material from the session and the task.

We usually ask the client, 'Do you think that another appointment would be helpful?' and if the answer is yes we ask them when they would like to come back. This level of choice is interesting, since clients often choose longer gaps between appointments than we would imagine. The date and time is set before the task so that the end of the session is not taken up with negotiating days and times and the task is the last part of the session.

The task

The notion of a task in Solution Focused Therapy is very different than in other forms of therapy. First, there is no expectation that the client will undertake any task. Clients modify or ignore a task when it doesn't fit for them and it could be argued that the therapist gave an inappropriate task, rather than the family failing at it. Instead, a task is an invitation to think about something, experiment with some new behaviour or notice existing successful behaviours. The task or home-work assignment is couched in the client's own language and its nature is determined by the client's own goals of therapy, their existing successes in this area, and their willingness or motivation (taken from the scaling questions) to make further changes. The task may be metaphorical, behavioural, supportive or something even more vague. Tasks help to continue the process of change. They help to focus clients on looking for areas of strengths and on exceptions.

The task will depend on the answers to the Miracle Question, exception question and scaling questions. For instance, someone who has given very specific answers to the Miracle Question or is asking for something concrete and gives a good detailed breakdown of the next steps and who is confident of achieving this, or who has some exception behaviours that help and who scores highly on motivation scales, will usually respond to a concrete 'doing' task, e.g., 'spend 10 minutes talking about anything but work to your partner'.

Conversely, someone who is vague in response to the Miracle Question, who is unable to give a picture of the next steps on a scale and who is low on motivation and confidence should only be given a gentle task such as: 'Notice what's happening that you would like to keep happening'; or 'We'd like to think about things more and we'd like you to think about things too so we can talk about this next time'.

Between these two extremes are infinite tasks in response to varying confidence, motivation answers and concrete/vague goals. The therapist tries to match the information gleaned from the session with a task that will be salient and make sense to the client.

The task is the last stage in a first session. The techniques described here give the beginning therapists a 'map' to follow to help him stay as solution focused as possible. All sessions are different and the order of questions, timing and pace and use of compliments, humour and self vary from therapist to therapist. We can now move on to discuss task design at greater length.

Exercise

Ask a colleague to role-play a client and try the Miracle Question, relationship and scaling questions. Swap roles and experience these questions first hand. Consider how pacing can affect these questions. Consider if your usual focus is on solutions and the future or problems and the past. Consider which techniques you have used already and which would be the easiest to adapt to your work setting. Re-read the getting started section and the basic assumptions of Solution Therapy. What influence would these make to your clinical work with clients (if any)?

4

Session 1 case example

Stuart, aged 34, is unemployed and referred by his GP for help with 'anxiety and panic attacks'. As always the first session is focused on how the client would like their life to be rather than what has gone wrong in the past. The therapist suspends any assumptions about the diagnosis in the referral letter, how difficult or easy the case seems to be on paper or how to help the client until they tell us about these issues.

We are often asked 'Are there any client groups that Solution Therapy will not work with?'. Our answer is, 'We don't know if we can be helpful until we've completed the initial interview.' The questions themselves serve the purpose of assessment and treatment.

Clients are all individuals and although we will see people who have the same diagnosis, in each case they will have different goals for themselves and will have thought about different solutions. Although we may see two people with a diagnosis of depression, they will want to work on the problem in different ways and have different expectations of a satisfactory outcome. Similarly, two people who are diagnosed with eating disorders will not necessarily have the same objectives as each other. We try to move away from labelling as much as possible, because in our experience the labels tend to influence what we see.

Therefore, Stuart will enter the room and meet a therapist who tries to suspend any pre-conceptions about him, and has tried to resist developing any hypothesis about him or the causes of his problem. This has the effect of ensuring that Stuart is involved in every stage of the development of any ideas in a genuine collaborative relationship. This also allows the therapist to come from a position of genuine curiosity.

Session 1

TH: 'Hello Stuart, my name is. . . . We're going to talk together for an hour or so. Towards the end of the session I'll take a short break of 5 or 10 minutes to think about what's been said and then I'll come back and share my thoughts with you. Is that OK?'

CL: 'Yeah sure.'

TH: 'OK Stuart, so what's brought you here today?'

CL: 'Well, my GP sent me.'

TH: 'So, what's led to your GP sending you here?'

CL: 'Well, I've been having panic attacks and feeling anxious for the last 2 years since I was in a bad car crash. This is really affecting me. I find it really difficult to drive now and I even get panic attacks in Tesco's for some reason. The medication I was on wasn't making a difference so my GP sent me to see you.'

TH: 'So, how can I help?'

CL: 'I'm not sure. I'd just like to be able to live a normal life again and not have all this to bother about.'

TH: 'So what difference will that make to you, when you don't have to worry about this any more, how will that help you?'

CL: 'Well, I can get on with my life, I'd feel happier. At the moment, every time I walk out of the door I feel awful and it has got so bad I just don't want to go out. And that's what I've come here to sort out.'

TH: 'I'm going to ask you a rather odd question, takes a bit of imagination, have you got a good imagination?'

CL: 'Yeah, I think so.'

TH: 'OK, suppose you leave the session today and you go home and this evening you go to bed and go to sleep. While you are sleeping, a miracle happens, and all the problems that you brought here today are solved, just like that, they're gone but you don't know this because you are still asleep. When you wake up tomorrow morning, what will be the first thing that you will notice that will tell you something must have happened in the night, everything is different?'
(Miracle Question)

CL: 'I'd feel happy.'

TH: 'What will you be doing differently that will tell you that you are happy?'
(Changing a vague feeling statement into an action statement.)

CL: 'Well, I'll feel like it's worthwhile getting up.'

TH: 'And when you get up, what will you do?'

CL: 'I suppose I'd go downstairs, have breakfast with the kids.'

TH: 'That would be different?'

CL: 'Yeah, normally I wait till the wife's sorted them out before I go down because I'm just so overloaded at the moment. I get this feeling of real dread and I'm too busy planning the day, like I'll have to go to the shops at three in the afternoon and at eight in the morning I'm already feeling rough about it and planning everything. While I'm doing all that I can't cope with the kids. I'm so fed up with it all. It's been like this too long.'

TH: 'That sounds really tough for you. After this miracle, how would that be different?'
(Re-orienting the client to solutions rather than problems.)

CL: 'I wouldn't be planning ahead. I'd be able to go to the shops without thinking about it and without getting so tensed up. I wouldn't have to avoid anyone at breakfast.'

TH: 'So how would you be instead?'

CL: 'I'd feel more relaxed. I'd go out more often than I do at the moment and I wouldn't be so ratty with my wife.'

TH: 'So how would you be if you weren't ratty?'

CL: 'We'd be talking more about anything other than how I feel, we'd be in each other's company more rather than avoiding each other.'

TH: 'What else will be different Stuart?'

CL: 'I'd be going out for a drive because I wanted to, I'd do the shopping without feeling I'd pass out at the checkout counter.'

TH: 'What else?'

CL: 'That's about it really. If I could do even the shopping bit that would be something.'

TH: 'What would your wife notice that would tell her a miracle had happened to you?'
(Relationship question.)

CL: 'We'd be talking more rather than fighting. I think I'd be prepared to listen to her because she's got a lot to cope with at the moment.'

TH: 'What difference do you think that will make to her?'

CL: 'I think it would make her feel that I'm recognizing that she's there and I think that she might be a bit more responsive to me instead of jumping down my throat.'

TH: 'In what way will she be more "responsive"?'

CL: 'She'd smile more and give me a hug, and we'd sit together more on the sofa watching television, all the things we used to do.'

TH: 'What else would she notice that would tell her that a miracle has happened to you?'

CL: 'She'd see me get over the panic attacks. If this was a real miracle I'd be back at work again.'

TH: 'Sounds like being back at work again is something you really want to do, that it'd make a big difference, how would that help?'

CL: 'I'd be bringing in some money, I probably wouldn't have so much time on my hands to worry about everything, we wouldn't be under each other's feet and I'd be able to take her out again.'

TH: 'That sounds like you'd really like that to happen.'

CL: 'Yeah, but I know I can't do any of that until I know I won't have any more of these attacks.'

TH: 'What else do you think she'd notice?'

CL: 'Well, I can't think about anything else, that's about it.'

TH: 'Do you have children Stuart?'

CL: 'Yeah, we've got two boys and a girl.'

TH: 'How old are they?'

CL: 'Greg is the oldest one, he'll be 9 in 2 months' time and Jake's six. Emma was born 5 months ago.'

TH: 'Right, what do you think they would notice about you that would tell them "something's different about dad today"?'

CL: 'Well, the first thing they'd notice is I wouldn't be shouting at them so much.'

TH: 'What would they see you doing instead?'

CL: 'I'd take them out more, I used to enjoy going to the park and all that. They are always asking me to take them somewhere and I'm always saying no.'

TH: 'So that would be really nice for them if you started taking them out more?'

CL: 'Yeah, they'd love it, especially Greg, he was always around me. We used to do a lot together before the accident and I don't think he really understands why I've changed. My wife says that he often asks what's wrong with me and she tells him "your dad's got a lot of problems on his mind". So I'd really like to be different with him, with all of them actually.'

TH: 'So you'd be taking the kids out, doing stuff with them, going out more on your own, talking more with your wife and at some point you'd have a job. You'd be able to go shopping and driving.'

CL: 'Yeah, that's all I want.'

TH: 'So, Stuart, are there any times when you notice parts of this miracle happening already, even in some small way?' (Exception question.)

CL: 'Well I drive already, I have to, but I feel panicky and when it gets too bad I just pull the car over and get out. Sometimes I'll leave it there and pick it up the next day.'

TH: 'So how do you do that, how do you get yourself to drive at the moment even though it's tough?'

CL: 'I don't know, I just make myself I guess?'

TH: 'How do you do that?'

CL: 'I don't know, I just have to do it. I suppose I'm not so bad at these times.'

TH: 'So what do you suppose you're doing at these times when it's not so bad? How come?'

CL: 'I'm not sure.'

TH: 'So something's happening or you're doing something right, even though you can't put your finger on it yet.'
(Indirect compliment.)

CL: 'Yeah, I suppose so, I wish I knew what I was doing so I could do it all the time.'

TH: 'Which other parts of the miracle have you noticed happening?'

CL: 'Well I have to go shopping because my wife can't manage the shopping and the kids on her own, so I have to go with her.'

TH: 'How do you get yourself to do that?'

CL: 'Well I know that if I run away, then she has to handle it all on her own and this makes me feel ashamed so I make myself stay. Sometimes when it's really bad, I'll sit in the car and wait for her.'

TH: 'Are there any times when you've surprised yourself, maybe expected a panicky feeling but something else happened?'
(Exception finding question.)

CL: 'Yeah, funnily enough, I don't always have a panic attack when I'm shopping.'

TH: 'Really, what do you think is happening at those times that makes a difference?'

CL: 'That's a tough one.'

TH: 'Yeah it is.'

CL: 'I think it's probably if I'm thinking about something else. Or sometimes the kids take some handling at the checkout and I'm too busy dealing with them. Before I know it we're in the car on the way home.'

TH: 'That's interesting. So if you are thinking about something else or are involved in something else, you don't have a panic attack?'

CL: 'I suppose so, I'd never thought about it that way before.'

TH: 'Are there any times when your wife notices that you're handling things a bit better?'

CL: 'Yeah, she notices every time when I don't have a panic attack, I think she's waiting for it to happen.'

TH: 'What difference does this make to your wife?'

CL: 'If things go OK in the supermarket it usually means there's no tension on the way home, we're getting on better and that normally carries on in the house.'

TH: 'So it makes quite a bit of difference?'

CL: 'Yeah, it's quite a relief.'

TH: 'On a scale of 0 to 10, where 0 was this problem at its worst and 10 is where you would like your life to be, where would you say you are at the moment?'
(Where are you now? Scaling question.)

CL: 'I'd say between 3 and 4.'

TH: 'So what would you say you have been doing that has got you to between 3 and 4?'

CL: 'Well, the fact that it doesn't happen all the time and that sometimes when it does happen it's not always that bad and on those occasions I never actually pass out or anything but I sort of stay with it.'

TH: 'How will you know, Stuart, that you have got to between 4 and 5, one small step nearer to 10?'

CL: 'If I didn't have these panic attacks any more.'

TH: 'That sounds like it's a big step, like maybe it's nearer 8 or 9.'
(Negotiating small achievable steps with the client.)

CL: 'Yeah, I suppose it is a way off.'

TH: 'So, Stuart, what would tell you that you've taken a small step further on?'

CL: 'If I could stay with them more and not give in.'

TH: 'How do you suppose you'll do that?'

CL: 'I don't know, maybe go more often so I get used to it, not let myself avoid it, try not to plan it in advance.'

TH: 'Can you think of anything else that will help you to do this?'

CL: 'Yeah, if I can distract myself more and talk to myself that may help.'

TH: 'What would tell your wife that you had moved just one point up?'
(Relationship based scaling question.)

CL: 'She'd say, if I did the kids' tea or something she'd think I was improving.'

TH: 'I've got another scaling question Stuart. On a scale of 0 to 10 where 0 is where all you're prepared to do is hope and pray that this problem will go away, and 10 is that you will do anything you think will help to sort out this problem, where are you on that scale?
(Motivation scale.)

CL: '10. I really want to get this sorted out.'

TH: 'So you really want to get this sorted out, this is really important to you?'

CL: 'Yeah, definitely.'

TH: 'OK, one more scaling question. On a scale of 0 to 10, where 10 is that you're really confident that you can sort this out, and 0 is that you don't think you'll ever make a dent in this, how confident would you say you are?'

CL: 'About 4 or 5.'

TH: 'What would need to happen to make you feel a little more confident?'

CL: 'If I could see myself sticking at it a little more than I do now. I think that would make me feel like I've got some control over this.'

TH: 'I'm going to take a break in a minute, but before I do that is there anything else that you can think of that we haven't talked about or that is important and you think I need to know?'

CL: 'No, well, I'd really like to know how come sometimes I get the panics and at other times I don't. That really bothers me because if I knew what it was, I could do it all the time.'

TH: 'OK, I'll think about that and about everything else that we've talked about during the last 45 minutes and I'll come back and share my thoughts with you in about 5 or 10 minutes, is that OK?'

CL: 'Fine.'

Because Stuart has exceptions to his panic attacks but does not know how come, the message revolves around a notice task to gain some more information about what he is doing at these times when the panics aren't happening.

TH: 'Despite things being very difficult for you at the moment, I'm really impressed, Stuart, at the amount of thought, hard work and energy you have given to this situation. You want to be different, to get in control of these panic attacks and you can see that that would make a big difference to you and a big difference to your family as well. It's clear to us that you think about the effect of this on them as well.'
(Compliments/acknowledging and validating.)
'Because you've said that there are times when you don't have panic attacks and you really want to understand more about why that is, and because you are high on your scale of wanting to sort this out (you said you were at 10) we would like to suggest ...'
(Bridging statement.)
'... that you notice all the times you manage to handle these panics more effectively and how come so that we can talk about it next time.'
(Task.)

Change does not always occur during the session, but the questions once asked cannot be retracted and tend to intrigue clients and provoke curiosity. Inherent in the therapist's questions is the suggestion that the client may have more control over difficulties than he gives himself credit for. When exceptions exist, but the client is not sure what happens to cause them, the task is one which invites them to go out into the world and investigate what is happening in more detail.

5

Intervention tasks

Learning objectives

By the end of this chapter, the reader should have a basic understanding of tasks, their development in behavioural approaches and use in varied Family Therapy models. Their subsequent adaptation to Solution Focused Therapy is discussed. The reader should understand the different intents behind solution focused tasks as compared with other therapy models. At the end of the chapter we will provide a primer of the kind of tasks often used in solution focused work. This is intended to stimulate practitioners but individuality and spontaneity are important in task construction.

Where did tasks come from?

Tasks developed through work by Behavioural Therapists in the 1950s. They evolved a (psycho-educational) method to ensure that clients undertook exercises that the therapists believed would help them to overcome the difficulties they were presenting. Tasks were a practical *in vivo* exercise which moved away from the world of psychoanalysis which emphasized the untying of mental knots inside an analytic session. The emphasis changed from 'think about' to 'go out and do'.

Early tasks were concrete common sense and enforced. An example would be instructing a client with agoraphobia to, first, imagine walking out of the door to the end of the garden (covert conditioning) and apply relaxation techniques. Once the task is completed the therapist goes on to issue step-by-step instructions on continuing to imagine and then engage in feared activities. This systematic de-sensitization allowed the clients to, gradually, overcome their anxieties by rehearsing in the real world. Behavioural programmes were generated to deal with diagnostic groups, e.g., phobias, panic attack, etc., and the same general tasks were used for each client belonging to such a group.

Milton Erickson, American Psychiatrist and father of hypnotherapy, used metaphor, story telling and trance-induced instructions to make a link between an imaginary 'successful outcome' and the client's own experience. These tasks are discussed in *Uncommon Therapy: The Psychiatric Techniques of Milton H. Erickson MD* (Haley, 1973). His tasks were, therefore, varied, ranging from direct behavioural instructions to 'vague' or hypnotic suggestions. Erickson increased the potential for success with his tasks by ensuring they were individualized to the clients' particular complaint, rather than general prescriptions and took into account their personality traits, dislikes and view of the world. As an example of concrete tasks for giving up smoking in a client who disliked exercise, he stated 'What I want you to do is to place your cigarettes in the attic of your house and the matches in the basement and that is where they are to remain.'

A more metaphorical example of Erickson's treatment of a young man who thought he was Jesus. The man resided in a large psychiatric hospital and did not take part in any therapeutic activities. Erickson approached him and engaged him in conversation, eventually commenting that, 'I believe you are interested in carpentry?'. Because of his world view, the man agreed and Erickson invited him to join the woodwork therapy class, which the client did.

A keystone of Erickson's therapy was the respect he held for his clients, believing each had the resources and capabilities to resolve their presenting difficulties. These examples appear simplistic but Erickson was a very skilled communicator and spent time understanding how the client saw the world. His tasks used the client's way of looking at the world (being Jesus) to undermine the problem (not having to relate to other people). This, in itself, was quite a revolutionary departure, as other theories' emphasis was, primarily, changing clients' outlooks directly as a way of solving problems, whereas Erickson believed that difficulties could be resolved without recourse to such fundamental measures.

The practical educational and catalytic effect of tasks appealed to Family Therapists in the 1950s and 1960s. Salvador Minuchin, who developed Structural Family Therapy, used tasks extensively (Minuchin, 1974). He would instruct families to argue together in his sessions so that he could observe the interaction with the intention of understanding the pattern between them. He then made practical suggestions such as, 'talk together more about this for 10 minutes only, three times a week until we next meet, but don't raise your voices'. His intent was to promote more structured communication to diffuse conflict. He still expected families to actually carry out these tasks regularly as prescribed. His tasks took people beyond their ordinary (and, sometimes, dysfunctional or habitual) experiences, teaching them a new way of relating. He believed change occurred in the session as a result of such exercises and tasks. He also made use of 'live supervision teams' that observed from behind a one-way screen. This technology allowed the development of Family Therapy since supervision of a session could be immediate, when the therapist needed it.

The theory behind Minuchin's therapy included an idea that families could be divided into 'sub-systems', i.e., grandparents, parents, older siblings, younger siblings. Each of these separate systems should have authority according to their place in the family hierarchy. He believed problems occurred when inappropriate alliances crossed the necessary boundaries in a family, or if the boundaries between these systems were too rigid. For example, parents should not discuss their sex life with their children (boundaries too loose) nor should they refuse to discuss anything of emotional value with their children (boundaries too rigid). A mother may choose a special child to help her in the home because father was away a lot. In Minuchin's eyes, this could result in the child developing symptoms such as depression, anorexia, school refusal, etc., and he would locate the causes of these symptoms in this 'distortion' of the family structure. Tasks would, then, be set to re-align the family, e.g., 'You have to woo your wife back, Mr Smith, because she isn't sure whether she is married to you or your daughter. So spend an hour together each night, without the children, planning the next day.' Another example would be, 'Somehow, your son has got the idea that he is married to your wife, not you. The two of you must be strong together in order to help him grow out of this. For this reason, for the next week, whatever discipline you need to give him must be backed up by the other partner completely.'

In summary, Minuchin gave tasks aimed at re-aligning the family boundaries. He believed in an ideal 'healthy family' as a pattern to work towards. Minuchin would say that having these boundaries clear was essential to the healthy functioning of both the family and its members.

Therapists, Weakland, Fisch, Bodin and Watzlawick, formed a group of 'Strategic Therapists' influenced by Erickson based in Palo Alto, California, and called the Mental Research Institute (MRI). They had an interesting way of understanding clients' difficulties. They believed that the client's *attempted solution* contributed more to maintaining the problem than the problem itself. The therapists focused on the problem and the patterns of interaction surrounding it (when, where, how, who was involved, what did you do next, what did your son say?). This detailed interviewing style would produce information that would help the therapist understand each member's contribution to the problem. Tasks were then developed to change, break or interrupt the usual pattern of interaction around the difficulty. For example, a naughty boy who misbehaves is given a smack. He still misbehaves and so he is sent to bed. He still misbehaves and he has his pocket money withdrawn, and so on. The parent would see each reaction as an attempt to solve the problem. The MRI team would see each step as more of the same punishment. They would develop a task to help the parents break this pattern. They would instruct the parent to reward good behaviour rather than punish bad (Watzlawick, Weakland and Fisch, 1974).

More controversially, the Strategic School regarded some families as so 'stuck' that the therapist must regard these cases as a 'battle' and change families, using whatever means possible. On occasion, they would deliver 'paradoxical tasks' to try and push the family in one extreme direction, hoping they would go in the other. For example, with a case where the wife called out continuously for reassurance from her husband, the paradoxical intervention may include the instruction, 'You need to call out for your husband even more'. 'We feel that you must call after your husband more and become more dependent than you are.' This instruction provides a situation where, if the wife calls out more, it is under instruction to do so and the behaviour is, therefore, controllable by her, and if there is less calling out, that is what the family came to solve. Unlike Salvador Minuchin's tasks, which were mainly explained to the family, Strategic Therapists used mysterious instructions that they never explained to clients, since doing so would lessen the impact. It is these more manipulative elements of Strategic Therapy that keep therapy brief, but may have led it to become less acceptable today.

The most influential model in the 1970s in family work was Systemic Family Therapy. It overtook structural and strategic work because of a fluid, gentle and respectful style. Initially developed in Italy it became known as the Milan approach. Its main protagonists were Pallazolli *et al.* (1978), all of whom were influenced by the work of Gregory Bateson (1972). This model took its name from their interest in expanding on Minuchin's original focus (the family) to look at the effects of wider social systems on individuals, couples and families. They were also more interested in how each member of the family saw a given situation and the differences in meaning each member would bring. They would be interested not just in the role of the family members in problems, but the role of social institutions (schools, the work place) and the issues of race and gender.

Originally working with anorexic families from all over Italy the team developed longer breaks between sessions (partly because of the distance families had to travel). They then found this had a useful therapeutic effect and would see families less frequently. They would see anyone who the family thought would be helpful to invite and this often included extended family members and friends. They developed an approach based on:

1. Hypothesizing
2. Circularity
3. Neutrality.

Hypothesizing

A number of ideas are generated through discussion as a team prior to the session. These varied interpretations of 'Why now?' and, 'What role does the family, school, culture, etc., play in this difficulty?' are discussed by the team. A complex family tree of 'genogram' is generated to highlight the possible patterns and 'myths' that may be passed around in this family and so influence the family's beliefs about the world.

Circularity

Once the varied hypotheses are generated the therapist asks questions to check out the fit of these ideas with the family. The questions used are 'circular questions'; that is, they are asked in a circular fashion of each of the clients in turn in order to build up a picture of each member's view of the situation and to interest them in the differences between these views, and perhaps help them to adopt a new picture thus reducing the need for the symptom.

For example, a mother may believe she is too hard on her children. The therapist starts with her and picks up this belief, 'So how do you think you do with the kids?'. He then asks the eldest son, 'How do you think your mum does with your brother?'. He then asks the brother, 'How do you think your mum is with the eldest?', and 'How do you think your brother is to your mum?', etc. These questions invite different views and also are 'gossiping' or 'triadic' questions. That is, they ask one member of the family to comment on the other two. Answers such as, 'Mum is all right with me and John', 'She's not as bad as she thinks but John could be a little nicer to mum', open up possibilities. 'Where do you think that your wife got the idea that she wasn't good with the kids when they say they are happy?'. The therapist simply becomes interested in these possibilities and asks each member in turn for their comments and ideas about this new information.

Other questions such as 'hypothetical questions', e.g., 'If the children's grandmother was here, would she agree with you or your kids about your parenting?'. Certainly, primary exponents of circular questioning, such as Karl Tomm and Peggy Penn, use a lot of creativity.

Neutrality

The family should leave the room feeling that they had equal time and that the therapist behaved similarly to each of them. This differs from Structural Therapy, where Minuchin may side exclusively with a family member in order to increase their stature within a 'dysfunctional' family system.

In terms of intervention design, Systemic Therapists developed 'messages' rather than tasks aimed at drawing together the families different meanings and inviting further discussion and thought. The Milan team developed an idea of 'positive connotation' whereby the pressure families feel under to solve the problem is lessened by the suggestion that the symptom helps the family in some way. At one stage Pallazoli *et al.* felt that this type of intervention (which is in itself a mild paradox) could be invariably prescribed. For example, 'We were interested in your ideas that you were a bad mother since your kids and husband feel that you are helpful to them and care for them. We don't know if you got this idea from your mother or someone else sold you this idea but we're wondering if it's helpful. Certainly, you having these doubts and feeling down has allowed you to get positive feedback from your family and be recognized and cared for by them for a change so we think you shouldn't change too quickly until you can work out how this can happen without you feeling depressed.'

Systematic Therapists do not believe in a 'blueprint for a perfect family', unlike Minuchin. They believe that what is 'right' for one family may be different for another. They have moved away from concrete tasks to messages designed to challenge the meaning of a problem.

The risks with the approach include practitioners becoming preoccupied with their particular hypotheses and asking clusters of complex questions about meaning or the influence of 'family myths' on behaviour when the family is simply searching for the most direct solution to what they perceive as a straightforward problem. The family's experience may then become that they are working at a different level to the therapist and this can undermine the therapeutic alliance between the therapist and the family. The family may not be as preoccupied with social issues and outside influences as the therapist. The therapist can see himself as having a political or educational role when there is no overt contract with the family to indulge in this kind of activity, however appropriate.

Tasks have been used to good effect in the various schools of Behaviour Therapy and Family Therapy. Tasks can be divided into behavioural instructions to carry out 'homework' prescribed in order to introduce new information or behaviour to the client. They can be concrete prescriptions to arrest an existing problem behaviour or interrupt a pattern. Finally, they may take the form of messages intended to invite the client to think more about an issue, or challenge their existing beliefs, helping them move on. Tasks are effective in helping clients change. Solution Therapy uses tasks and interventions and some knowledge of their development and adaptation by other models is useful to the Solution Practitioner. Solution Therapy uses some of these broad interventions but often in a different context and for a different purpose.

The use of interventions in Solution Focused Therapy

As we discussed briefly during the stages of a first session, interventions in Solution Focused Therapy derived directly from the work that goes on in the session and are the result of collaboration between the therapist and his client(s). We give a task since it is a simple way of summarizing, and also clients usually expect therapists to make some suggestions which could result in progress. Some of de Shazer's early tasks were influenced by the techniques of strategic therapy; however, the solution focused tasks are not delivered from an expert stance, nor is there an expectation that clients should necessarily do them. We trust clients to take what they need from a given intervention or session and make the most creative use of it. Interventions are seen as complementary to the client's own creativity. They may make use of what is suggested or may alternatively adapt or ignore it either because they have decided it is not relevant or something else is more appropriate. The relationship between the therapist and client, even in intervention design, can be seen to be an equal one. We usually 'suggest' actions and give our rationale to the family about why we think they might be useful. Also we may 'suggest' a task and add the phrase, 'but maybe you will find another way of doing this that we wouldn't come up with'. We may also develop 'multiple tasks' such as 'you could do this, this or this or any combination of the three . . .'. The aim is to give clients as many chances to be as 'successful' as possible. Traditional tasks are often 'either/or', in that the family is restricted to doing what the therapist says exactly or failing in some way. Ben Furman suggests that an important part of successful therapy is ensuring no-one 'loses face' or feels that they failed. Solution tasks minimize the chances to fail. For this reason we will not usually directly ask the clients if they have completed a task or not in session two. The reasoning behind this is that if you ask families whether they have done the task and they haven't, this can add to their feeling of failure; and if they have done it and it's been a success, they'll tell you anyway. The usefulness of an intervention usually becomes apparent during the session so we don't need to ask.

In summary, unlike structural therapy, we wouldn't deliver the tasks from an 'expert stance' and would give clients some opportunity to do something else. Unlike systemic therapy (of the Milan era) we wouldn't use 'positive connotation' since why accredit something that the family wants to be rid of with usefulness? The slight paradoxical nature of this technique clashes with the solution focused ideas of equality and honesty. Unlike some strategic interventions the aim of the task is always revealed; there is nothing 'up the therapist's sleeve' and no covert intent. Again, paradoxical ideas carry information of which the family is not aware, and so would not play a part in solution focused thinking. Solution Therapy, however, does carry some of the directness and accessibility of structural work, the curiosity and openness to new ideas of Systemic Therapy and has elements of the creativity involved in strategic work.

Intervention design

The major considerations in a team's intervention design are:

1. Does the task take into account the client's goal in terms of their answers to the Miracle Question?
2. Does the task realistically match the client's willingness to do, confidence, etc., scales?
3. Are there concrete exceptions to the problem which may be built on or explored further? Does the client regard himself as being in control of these exceptions?
4. Is there anything from the session that the client was particularly interested in, curious about or surprised by, or seemed particularly relevant that may be useful.

The intervention should use as much of the client's language as is appropriate, especially words or phrases that are unusual or idiosyncratic (for example, our clients talk about 'off the rails days' or 'doing my pieces'). This helps the client to feel genuinely heard and makes the message personal to him.

Tasks

Notice tasks

It may be safer to send clients back out into the world to do some kind of 'experiment' which involves them 'noticing' anything that happens that gets them closer to any desired result if:

1. clients are very low on a 0 to 10 scale about willingness to do
2. they are vague in their idea of a 'miracle' and find it hard to work out what the next step along a scale will look like
3. they want somebody else to change instead of them; or
4. there are few exceptions which the client does not see as significant
5. they are, clearly, overloaded and working to the limit to contain things
6. you are still not sure about the client's goal or what type of intervention fits.

Noticing tasks do not ask the client to do anything physically different but provide more information and encourage the client to be more focused on what helps. Clients often come to therapy focusing on difficulties in their life and cannot see what they are doing that helps or improves things. The nature of the public's idea of 'help' or 'treatment' also encourages people to describe, in detail, the seriousness of the problem and its effects. This creates an unbalanced view of the individuals since they are often doing things which are good for them or may even solve the problem if they continue them for longer. Solution Therapy encourages the client to value their own attempts to solve a difficulty. Notice tasks orient the client to think more about what helps and about their potential. 'Because you have said that you do have better days but are not sure how, what we would like you to do is to notice anything that happens that you want to keep on happening that makes a day a little better for you so we can talk about it next time.'

Less specific versions of this task are called, by de Shazer, 'formula first session tasks' in his book *Keys to Solutions in Brief Therapy* (1985, p. 137). 'Between now and next time we meet, I would like you to observe, so that you can describe to me next time, what happens in your family/life/relationship that you want to continue to have happen' (de Shazer and Molnar, 1987).

They were used, regardless of diagnosis, in order to introduce a solution frame to clients to act as 'skeleton keys' that could unlock change in a wide variety of situations. These tasks are transferable and do not depend on the therapist being able to describe the problem or even (technically) know what it is. These tasks are, also, useful for clients whose response to the miracle or scale questions is vague or confused, or find it difficult to articulate their problem.

It occurs to us that, traditionally, therapy tended to focus on, 'What do you want to change?', in Solution Therapy you can also ask clients, 'What do you want to keep?', which reduces blame and points out positive qualities. This approach often pleasantly surprises families.

Prediction tasks

The therapist has a wider choice and may introduce a 'prediction task' or a more specific variation of the notice task if the client is:

1. more specific about how he wants his life to be;
2. perhaps, higher on the scales;
3. or interested in occasional exceptions he has identified.

Prediction tasks provide a slightly more structured opportunity for the client to think about what happens that affects his mood or behaviour and to introduce the idea of potential control. They invite clients to predict if the next day will be a 'good' or 'bad' day and see how accurate their prediction is and, 'How come?'. They can be used when clients have exception periods but feel they are random or out of their control: 'Because you have said good and bad days seem to be random occurrences, we would like you, before you go to bed each night, to predict whether the next day will be good or bad and on the following night account for the outcome before making a prediction for the following day.'

These tasks can encourage some degree of rehearsal by encouraging the client to consider possibilities for next day rather than, simply, taking it as it comes. This may in turn change the client's ability to cope with events that befall them. These tasks also allow the client to check out their assumptions about what affects them and to test it against how they actually feel.

They can be a stepping stone to asking the client the next time: 'When you predict a bad day, notice how you are able to turn it into a better one. What you do or what happens that makes a difference?' This attempts to place agency in the hands of the client rather than fate. These tasks are designed to help the client think about the events of his life as linked to his actions and, therefore, open up opportunities to act differently.

Specific notice tasks

These tasks are useful:

1. when you have detailed exceptions to the problem but a vague idea about how they come about;
2. when a client is low on 'motivation/willingness to do'.

For example, with a client who manages to avoid drinking, 'Notice what's happening (who is around, what are you doing/thinking/feeling, where you are, etc.) when you overcome the urge to drink', or for a client who wants to be more in control of their life by being calmer when being criticized at work, 'Notice what is happening at the times you do manage to accept comments from others and still manage to state your point of view calmly and clearly, rather than raising your voice or leaving'. These tasks can also be linked to scales, e.g., 'Notice what happens that moves you one point up the scale, e.g., from 4 to 5.'

Do something different tasks

When there is a detailed description of a particular process, for instance where couples report that they fight continuously and have been unable to change this, 'We've heard that you really want things to change and from what you've said you've been trying very hard, you would expect your efforts to make a difference. Having listened to you we also would have expected your attempts to have made a difference but for some reason, that neither of you or we understand, what you are doing isn't working enough so we would suggest that you go away from here and do something different, anything that maybe you haven't tried before and observe how this helps.' This task encourages people to become more creative in their attempts to break patterns of behaviour. Because it is generalized and the therapist has no part in suggesting what they actually do, any change can be attributed to the client themselves. If the clients then report change we would ask: 'How did you know this was the right thing to do?'; 'Did this come naturally or did it take some effort?', 'What did you learn about each other from doing this?', and 'What difference did it make?'.

A couple we worked with reported arguments over petty household issues that escalated to shouting pitch. Even though the couple knew this was pointless they still engaged in this process. We asked them to 'do something different; we don't know what it will be but experiment and we'll talk about it next time'. The couple returned to the next session and related that they had bought water pistols. During their next argument they squirted each other with water and they started to laugh and this broke up the argument. We could never have instructed the couple to behave in this manner or even dreamed that they would reach this solution. We are often reminded of clients' creativity as a result of these tasks. We later discovered that de Shazer had used a water pistol intervention regularly with couples in the early 1970s and our couple had independently reinvented it! (Correspondence with de Shazer by the authors, 1998).

Coping tasks

These tasks ask a client to consider how they cope with a situation, what is it that they are doing that helps them get through each day. They are used:

1. when clients are overwhelmed by their problems;
2. when they feel unable to act;
3. when they are very low on their 'where are you now scale' or 'willingness to do' scale (e.g., in the minus side of the scale);
4. with depression, suicidal thoughts or problems that they have no influence over, e.g., redundancy, relationship break-ups, terminal or debilitating illness, bereavement, etc.

They are not about to 'change' but are about survival. For example, with a man who felt suicidal because his marriage is breaking up against his will: 'Because things are really tough for you at present we'd like you to notice everything that happens that helps you to cope and get through the day.'

Randomization tasks

These tasks help clients determine a course of action when they have viable alternative options and cannot decide which to follow. For example, when a parent can't decide whether to shout in order to enforce bedtime or cajole the children into compliance: 'Because it is difficult to make a decision about this we would suggest that you toss a coin and if it's heads you shout and if it's tails you don't, and see which works best? Is it the first, the second or a mixture of both?' The tossing of a coin can also interrupt a pattern of indecisiveness and argument between couples and can avoid a power struggle by taking the responsibility of decision making away from either partner. For example, with a couple wishing to work together to cope with an over-bearing relative, 'if it's heads, your husband speaks to his mother on the phone, if it's tails, you do'.

Concrete tasks

These are specific tasks evolved when:

1. willingness to do is high;
2. when the problem is specific, e.g., 'we want to talk more and argue less';
3. when it is obvious from the content of the session that the clients want to do something active and the task presents itself.

For a couple who state that their 'miracle' would be to talk together more without arguing: 'Because you've said that you need to talk more without it becoming an argument, we would like to suggest that on three occasions each week (or as often as feels necessary) you set aside half-an-hour of uninterrupted time where we would like one of you to talk for 10 minutes about anything you think is important to you and the other partner is to listen and to show they are listening but cannot respond. At the end of the 10 minutes, take a break and make a drink, then reverse the roles. Finally, do something nice for the other person before retiring.' This ensures that each partner can say what they need to without the threat of an argument ensuing. Another example would be: 'Because you've said that spending time with your parents helps you control the voices we'd suggest that you do more of this.'

Because of the risk that concrete tasks take authority away from the client and can leave the client with the idea that success is due to the therapist and his intervention, it is vital that they are not dropped in at random. We only use them when we have checked out with the client that they would be useful, e.g., 'If we asked you to do something specific that we think might help with this would you be prepared to do it?'.

Pretend tasks

These tasks invite clients to pretend a 'miracle' has happened and act accordingly, observing the effect this has on their relationships. They are used when:

1. there is a detailed miracle picture in small behavioural terms, e.g., 'I'd be smiling more, getting up at eight instead of staying in bed, I'd shower before breakfast, get in touch with my friends more and go to play snooker occasionally, etc.';
2. willingness to do is high;
3. clients want to make change but don't know how to start.

For the above client: 'Because you've got a good idea about what this miracle would consist of we'd like you to pick three days at random and pretend the miracle has happened and notice what difference this makes to yourself and to the other people in your life; how are they different?'

The interface between 'pretending' and 'reality' is explored and blurred by this task. This sets up a positive cycle of behaviour where the client is unable to say where 'pretending' stops and 'reality' takes over. In families it is often useful to ask that the 'pretend day' is kept secret from the other members of the family and that they guess which day the client chose. Often the family will highlight positive behaviours on particular days and the 'miracle day' was totally different. You can even end up with a whole week of so called 'miracle days' when the client only 'pretended' once.

Ritual tasks

The use of rituals to resolve difficulties and to mark the end of stages in a person's life or development are a logical extension of our use of rituals to mark important events. They can be seen to link elements of controlled emotional catharsis with a prescribed behavioural task. They would be used:

1. when people's 'willingness to do' is high;
2. when they are preoccupied with an emotional issue which interferes with them moving towards their stated goals;
3. when dealing with issues around grief and loss.

For example, with a client who was made bankrupt and feels very angry towards the bank: 'Because it seems that you want to start afresh with your life but you are so angry about the past that you cannot concentrate on the things you would like to do, what we would like to suggest is that you put all the paper, letters from the bank, etc., into an envelope, make a bonfire in the garden and at a set time chosen by you, read each letter and burn it.'

With issues relating to physical or sexual abuse, it can be useful to suggest that the client: 'Write a letter to the person(s) involved stating your thoughts and feelings, read it and then destroy it in the most satisfying way imaginable.'

With grief, where clients feel they cannot move on because of unstated emotions, when it is respectful to do so, letter writing, with or without destroying it afterwards, may be useful: 'Because you have said that you never had the chance to say goodbye, what we would like to suggest is that you find a place or a time that will help you feel close to your father and write him a letter telling him what you feel you need to say.'

Each case is individual and the final element of the task may be to destroy the material, to keep it, to give it to a loved one, etc. Each part of the ritual is negotiated with the client: 'Will you feel OK about that or is there something else that would be more appropriate?' For children, an abundance of creative rituals and tasks exist. Clients can be asked to write down fears, anger, feelings, etc., and lock them away or give them to the therapist who locks them up, ritualistically, in a 'strong box' in the office (after the child has inspected the box, made it stronger, sealed it, etc.). This allows unwanted emotions to be kept safe. It, also, 'externalizes them' and we will cover this process of externalization as developed by White and Epsten (1990) later.

Tasks that utilize competitiveness

Most families have a natural competitiveness that can be used in both a positive and a negative way. These tasks aim to harness it positively. The decision about using these tasks is more to do with the sense the therapist has of the family culture.

Families in crisis, on occasion, seem to get stuck in patterns of mutual recrimination and hostility. Often, this may, simply, be a way of avoiding blame for a situation that evolved. In such families it may be useful to harness this competitive spirit. For example, with fighting couples, Insoo Kim Berg told us about a task that was developed by some Solution Therapists in Spain: 'We are prepared to bet that between now and the next session both of you will do something nice for the other, but we are also prepared to bet that whichever one of you does something nice, the other will not notice.' Keeping secret positive behaviour and asking others to look out for it harnesses competitiveness, and can also encourage teenagers and children to be inventive in their methods of doing something for the family in order to confound their parents: 'Do something nice for the other person but don't tell them what it is and we will talk about it next time to see if they have noticed.'

In a case we saw, father had been made redundant and the family had lost their accommodation. Son had, also, lost his job and had to move back home. They wanted to survive this as a family together but were so angry about the events that they would end up being sarcastic with each other. The intervention was:

> The events that have happened over the past few months have been a tremendous crisis for this family. Despite the fact that these things were out of your control and this has left you feeling, understandably, angry about the situation, you have realized that it is not helpful to take these things out on each other. Despite this crisis, which

would have torn many families asunder, Mum said that what she wants most of all is for you all to be able to see this through together and we are impressed with this as, clearly, you mean a lot to each other. Because you want to stick together, what we would like you to do is, between now and the next time we meet, on two or three occasions, do something quite small to show how much you appreciate another member of the family and, if you feel that someone has done something nice for you, do something in return, so that when you come back we can talk about it and note what happened and who has noticed.

Vague interventions

Sometimes, by the time of the intervention statement, the client still has not been able to answer the Miracle Question or scaling questions, or provide the therapist with the information to develop an intervention or strategy. To paraphrase de Shazer, 'what you get is what you get'. On these occasions, it may be most appropriate for both the therapist and client to go away and think a little more before the next session: 'Because you have said that things are confusing at the moment and you don't know how you would like things to be different and we are not sure yet how we can help. What we would like you to do is think a little more about the situation and we will do the same and we will talk together again next time.'

Summary

The reader will have been introduced to the role of therapeutic messages and tasks in differing Family Therapy models. Tasks in Solution Focused Therapy are less to do with therapists' initiated change and more to do with summarizing the session and amplifying successful behaviours. These tasks are matched to the client's goals, Miracle Question and scales.

Exercises

Consider the differences between Family Therapy models and Solution Therapy in their attitude towards tasks. Consider the conditions under which a 'vague task' would be warranted. Consider one of your own clients and develop a full intervention using compliments, bridge and solution focused task.

6

Session 2 and beyond:
What to say after you have said
'Hello again'

Learning objectives

By the end of this chapter, the reader will have been introduced to the stages of a second session of Solution Therapy. The concepts of 'relapse' and 'dependency' are addressed, and pacing according to the type of relationship you have with the client (visitor, customer or complainant) is explored. Common faults in technique are discussed.

Most trainees find the initial techniques of this approach are easy to apply. However, they often stumble in subsequent sessions and this is partly due to the comparative lack of material about how to conduct later sessions. Solution Therapy can be compared to a chess manual in which most participants write about the opening gambits, and not about the middle or end game.

The most important element in subsequent sessions is the therapist's ability to remain confident in the approach without losing rapport with the client. The space between sessions is characterized by 'experiment'.

Session two can essentially be divided into two components. First, the therapist interviews to elicit change between sessions. Second, to discover what else needs to be different for the client to settle for their life. Our experience in supervising role-play suggests that when clients report little change, or express further problems in session two, the therapist can panic, believe they are 'doing something wrong' or feel the client is 'too difficult', when in fact if they listened, slowed down their pace and remained curious, possibilities would emerge. Remaining patient, listening respectfully and not taking on too much responsibility for change is harder than it may appear.

The Solution Therapist listens to all of the material that the client brings to therapy initially with equanimity, 'If you can meet with triumph and disaster and treat those two impostors just the same' (Kipling, 1910). There is a tendency for practitioners to *prefer* certain answers than others or to *expect* positive change. If there is no immediate positive response from the client these expectations can lead to a cycle where the practitioner feels disappointed, tries harder to 'lead' the client into talking about positives ('Yes, but you did cope with this well.') and the client experiences the feeling that they haven't been heard. As we discussed before, once the therapist attempts to lead the client then the basic premises of the approach are lost behind an 'expert' stance. Instead, the Solution Therapist merely highlights or 'flags' positive changes that the client introduces to therapy.

We learned a great deal about how to proceed after session one from the team at the Brief Family Therapy Centre in Milwaukee, USA, during our residence there in Summer 1992.

Previously our ideas about session two were that we would start with an exploration about how the client got on with the task set in the first session. Doing so, however, creates the potential for clients to feel embarrassed if they;

1. haven't attempted it;
2. have not succeeded in producing any degree of positive change;
3. did not think it was relevant; or
4. had adapted the task in some way that suited them.

A Solution Focused philosophy, however, would maintain that a failure on the part of the client to comply with the task is, in fact, their way of educating the therapist about their own individuality and, in effect, what works with them. Families often discover a far more creative solution for themselves than the therapist, and the aim in session two is to help them express these successes even if they do not fit with the previous task. So, just as the first session does not start with hypothesizing about the nature of the problem, the second session does not start with a report on the homework task.

The opening stages of a second session conform to the simple nemonic EARS (explained below) followed by questions aimed at clarifying if change is enough and what else needs to happen? This is followed by questions to encourage the client to take the next steps toward their 'miracle' or by a decision to 'do something different'.

Elicit, amplify, re-state and start again (EARS)

EARS is a set of questions first developed by de Shazer *et al.* (1986) to uncover existing change.

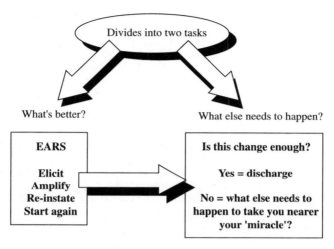

Fig. 6.1 Session 2 and beyond.

Elicit

Session two begins with the therapist asking, 'What's better?'. The rationale for this is the assumption that something must have changed. We can ask this question with confidence since we believe that change always occurs; 'Stability is an illusion created by the memory of an instant'. Things are better or worse since you last met but cannot be the same since new experiences will have occurred, however subtle, in the intervening period between sessions. We interview to discover difference, the days that were slightly better, the parts of a bad day that were not quite as bad, and are then curious about how these variations occurred. We also give agency for these changes to the client rather than to fate. The therapist, therefefore, breaks the week(s) down into days to get more information about differences: 'On the day we met what happened?'; 'How was the next day?'; 'What was Wednesday like?', etc. This process invites the client to look at each day realistically, and put into perspective the extent of positive experience. Clients often surprise themselves during this sequence, finding that a greater range of positive, as well as negative, experiences occurred than they initially remembered. Alternatively, the therapist can 'double scale' the week by asking the client: 'On a scale of 0 to 10, where 0 was the worst day and 10 was the best, what was the highest scoring day/hour, etc.?'; 'What was the lowest?'; 'What was different on the high scoring day?', etc.

Amplify

Clients often do not give themselves enough credit for changes and attempted solutions. These questions attempt to credit the client and value even small pieces of new behaviour as significant. They also introduce the idea of 'agency', that the client is responsible for change rather than a 'victim' of flukes, fate or the therapist. Amplifying introduces the link between the clients' actions and change. Techniques used include:

1. 'Flagging' change, which is essentially noticing it, e.g., the therapist non-verbally acknowledging a statement from the client with a raise of the eyebrow, leaning forward, noting it down, facial expression or saying 'really!', 'say that again'. This can be quite minimal to register with the client that you have heard that change has taken place and see it as important and noteworthy.
2. Questions designed to expand how change occurred and link the client as the protagonist of change such as: 'How did you know that was the right thing to do?'; 'How did you get yourself to do that?'; 'Did that come naturally or did it take a lot of hard work?'; 'You did what?'; 'When did you do this?'; 'Who or what was around that helped you make this change?'; 'How did that help?'; 'Who else noticed the better day?'; 'What was different for your wife, kids, workmates as a result of this?'; 'How will you get yourself to do more of this ?'; 'What did your wife, kids, workmates do differently as a result of you doing this?'; 'Was this new for you?'; 'How many times did this occur?'; 'What have you learned about yourself from this?'; 'What gave you the idea to do this?'; 'What did you think or say to yourself that helped you achieve this?'; Did you surprise yourself?' or 'Did you know you were capable of this?'; 'Who else do you think was surprised by what you've done?'.

The therapist is careful not to state 'do this' since again they would then be leading the client. If it is was as easy as that the client would have already achieved their goal without the therapist's involvement. The possibility of patronizing clients is minimized by a stance of genuine curiosity about positive change and a belief in the client's resources and ability to change. This stage implicitly empowers the client and the client describes what they will do more of rather than the therapist telling them what they should do. In a similar manner to multiple end-points in the first session, the more the client gets to talk about small pieces of change and how they were achieved, the more likely it is that the next step will naturally emerge.

Re-state

This ensures that the link between the client's actions and change is made. It indicates intent on behalf of the client (all be it possibly not recognized) and summarizes the positives. Re-stating links small changes to the achievement of the client's overall goal, their miracle picture: 'So you thought a lot about this and you really wanted to try out this idea of getting out more so you picked a day and visited your sister and she was pleased to see you', etc.

Also, from the field of Brief Therapy (particularly by the Mental Research Institute, Palo Alto, USA) comes the ideas of 're-framing', that is, the therapist providing a new emphasis to clients' descriptions of events. For example, a family describe their son as having 'tantrums' and the therapist introduces the idea that he is 'spirited'.

Start again

The therapist asks, 'What else has been better?', and continues with this sequence of questioning until the client can think of nothing else that is better.

EARS helps by giving the therapist a map to start the second session with. It is focused on discovering and expanding on positive change. With some clients this is enough; however, with most the changes they have attempted are only part of their 'miracle' and the therapist needs to clarify: 'Is this change enough?' and 'What else needs to happen?'

When EARS isn't enough

EARS isn't enough when the client still reports 'no change' ('Nothing was different at all'); or there is change but it is not enough ('My husband did talk more once but then gave up'); or where the change is not relevant ('We spoke more together and got on better but I still had a panic attack'). The therapist then needs to clarify with the client 'what needs to happen next to make things even a little better for you?'. He needs to check the client's position on their scales and get another picture of the next small step for them. He needs to consider whether the client's goal has changed since the last session by feeding back to them, 'Last time you said you wanted a, b and c. Is this something you still think would help?'. He may need to slow down and allow the client to: consider other options, 'What haven't you tried?', 'How do you imagine someone else would deal with this?', 'Is there anyone who could help you with this?'; and explore further exception periods, 'When you have had a problem similar to this in the past, how have you overcome it?', 'Is there some memory, thought or person that you can take to help you overcome this?', 'What ideas have you got about how to proceed?'.

It may be that the therapist has missed the client's goal which may be simpler and the 'no change' may be the client's educating the therapist that they, actually, want something specific, such as relaxation training, marriage guidance or referral to a doctor for a physical check up. 'What would really be helpful to you?', 'How can I help you with this a little more than I have been?' will try and access this. A 'no change' or 'things are worse' answer may mean that the client has tried the task or thought about the questions and this has altered the way he sees the problem. Again, Solution Therapists would not assume that the client was resistant or difficult but, simply, that this is the way things are and the client is educating him about the most direct route to his goal. In a second session of therapy, various scenarios are possible. We will discuss them in turn.

Change of the right kind and it's sufficient

On some occasions, clients report change has happened and, also, that the changes have been enough. In these situations, follow-up sessions lead to swift discharge. The therapist follows EARS, checks that the change has been enough, checks that the client is confident about 'keeping on track' and knows, in detail, what to do to continue to move forward. In Solution Therapy, such sessions may be shorter than the first sessions since, once this is established, and 'anything I have missed' has produced no further material, we are happy to end the session rather than prolong it for the sake of an arbitrary time limit. The two major activities of the therapist in session two are: (1) Interviewing to elicit change. (Since we know change happens, 'stability is an illusion created by the memory of an instant'.) This is encapsulated in the mnemonic EARS; and (2) Interviewing to discover what else needs to happen. This involves direct questions such as, 'Is this change enough?' and 'What else needs to happen to move you a little more towards your "miracle"?'. Re-scaling, checking the miracle and considering if there has been a change in goal. It may also involve the therapist in asking: 'Is this really helping?', or 'Is there anything I could do differently that you think would be more helpful to you here?'.

Basically, the therapist always returns to what Anderson and Goolishian call 'a position of now knowing'. The client is the expert and, perhaps, the most important question is, 'How can I really be helpful to you with this?'. The therapist does not take responsibility for the client's problem in this model; that would be presumptuous or patronizing. Instead, client and therapist embark, together, on a joint investigation into what would be helpful. It may also involve questions such as, 'Now you have tried all this and feel you cannot change your husband, what can you do to make things even a little better for yourself?'. We call these clusters of questions the 'non-miracle scenario'. If the 'miracle' really cannot happen or is out of a client's control, the therapist asks, 'While you are waiting for something to change, how can you look after yourself a little more?'. This can help the clients develop new and more achievable goals for themselves if there has been no change, someone else has to do the changing, or if they consider change is outside of their control.

7

Session 2 case examples

Following our initial session with Stuart (see Chapter 4), session 2 went as follows.

Therapeutic activity A

Eliciting change between sessions (elicit, amplify, re-state, start again)

TH: 'What's better?' (Elicit)

CL: 'Well, since I saw you I've had two "minor" panic attacks, but this time, instead of running away from them I decided to stay with them to see what would happen.'

TH: 'Really? You stayed with the panic attacks. How did you do that?' (Amplifying)

CL: 'It was tough, but I remembered our conversation and I had the idea that running away wasn't helping. Nothing had changed in the last two years and I needed to do something different.'

TH: 'Really? So you decided that this time you were going to do something different and what you did was stay with it. How did you do that? I am really curious.' (Re-stating)

CL: 'Well, I began thinking, "What's the worst that could happen to me?". I know that I can drive because I do it now and I can shop because I do it now. So I think, realizing that I don't always have these panic attacks, made me wonder "How come"?'

TH: 'OK, but what did you actually do, Stuart, when you were feeling panicky that helped you to stay there and in control.' (Amplifying)

CL: 'I was talking to myself. I told myself, "I can cope with this", and I also got involved with a conversation with my wife and that helped to take my mind off of it.'

TH: 'Right, so you are saying that talking to your wife helped to distract you from it and telling yourself that you can handle this, that helped you to stay in control. Is that right?' (Re-stating)

CL: 'Yeah.'

TH: 'What did you learn about yourself, Stuart, by doing this?' (Amplifying)

CL: 'That I can do it. That I can deal with feeling panicky and I don't have to run away.'

TH: 'So, was this tough for you to do this?'

CL: 'Bloody right. I wanted to run away, but what have I got to gain by doing that? I've been doing it for two years.'

TH: 'Sounds like you worked hard at this. What difference did it make to you?' (Amplify/Elicit)

CL: 'Ah, I feel more confident.'

TH: 'How does feeling more confident show itself?' (Elicit)

CL: 'Well, I've been driving more, taking my wife round her friends and the kids to their activities and I, actually, stayed in the supermarket with my wife on Friday.'

TH: 'Really, that's great. That's a big change.' (Amplifying)

CL: 'Yes it is. I couldn't do that a few weeks ago.'

TH: 'What would you say your wife has noticed that was different about you?' (Elicit)

CL: 'We're together, for a start, I'm not locked in some room somewhere. I'm calmer, not as tense around the house as I was.'

TH: 'Instead of being tense, what has she noticed about you?'

CL: 'I've been sitting down more with her, watching TV, just normal things. Asking about her and what's going on in her life, rather than talking about me and how I feel.'

TH: 'What difference has that made to her, do you suppose?'

CL: 'Well, she was getting really fed up with me, I think she'd had enough. I've been grumpy, didn't want to go out with her, had no time with the kids.'

TH: 'So, how are saying that is changed, Stuart?'

CL: 'Well, it's nice to see her smile a bit and be a bit warmer, we're getting on now.'•

TH: 'So, what would you say your children have noticed that would tell them there is something different about dad?'

CL: 'Well, Greg, the eldest one, he's noticed that I've been spending more time with him. I've been taking him out and actually enjoying it rather than leaving it to his mum, or feeling we had to come home early. In fact, he said, "Oh are you taking me dad?". I think he was a bit surprised.'

TH: 'So you surprised him.'

CL: 'Yes.'

TH: 'Did you surprise yourself as well or did you know you could do this?'

CL: 'I did surprise myself, actually' (laughing).

TH: 'What about the rest of your children. What do you think they noticed that was different about dad?'

CL: 'Well, Emma is just a baby, I don't think she'll have noticed anything but Jake, my youngest boy, I think he'll have noticed that dad's a bit happier this week and that I'm not as snappy with them.'

TH: 'So, what have you noticed that's different about Greg, Jake and Emma this week that tells you things are on track?'

CL: 'Well, for some reason they seem better behaved, less boisterous.'

TH: 'Really? What do you think you have done that's helped them become calmer?'

CL: 'Well, I think it's just that I've had more time for them and me and their mum have been getting on better.'

TH: 'I'm really impressed. You confronted two panic attacks and saw them through and you've noticed that things are better at home. You've been going out together to do the shopping, talking more and you say that talking to your wife helps take your mind off the panic feelings. You've been taking more time with the children and that's paid off too. That's a lot of change.' (Reinforcing)

CL: 'Well, when you add it all together I suppose it is a lot of change.'

TH: 'And these are the sort of changes that you are looking for, Stuart?'

CL: 'Yes, this is what I wanted to happen, I just didn't know how to make it happen.'

Therapeutic activity B

Questions that find out 'What else needs to happen?'

TH: 'So, what are you going to have to do to keep these changes happening?'

CL: 'I need to keep calm during the panic attacks, talk to someone, remind myself that I can do it and keep spending time with my wife and kids. I think that's good for us.'

TH: 'On a scale of 0 to 10, how confident are you that you can keep this going?'

CL: '7 or 8 because I feel good but it's early days.'

TH: 'Can you think of anything that would make you a little bit more confident?'

CL: 'Yeah, just keep going. Keep doing what I'm doing, I know it's going to take time.'

TH: 'Remember that other numbers thing we talked about?'

CL: 'What, the where am I?'

TH: 'Yeah, where are you on that today, do you think, between 0 and 10?'

CL: 'About 6.'

TH: 'What would take you to 7?'

CL: 'Just sticking at it; more of what I'm already doing.'

TH: 'Going out, spending time with your wife, telling yourself you can do it, and so on?'

CL: 'Yes.'

TH: 'So, do you suppose that you know what to do now to move you up the scale? Or do you need another session with me?'

CL: 'I know what to do now, I don't need to see you again, but perhaps I could call you if I need to?'

TH: 'Sure, that's no problem. Is there anything else, Stuart, that we have missed or that you think is important that we need to talk about?'

CL: 'Not really, I think I have said it all.'

TH: 'I'm going to take a break now for about five minutes to think about what we have talked about and I'll come back and share my thoughts with you about this.'

There has been change and the therapist has been able to stay with EARS for most of the session. The responses to, 'What else has to happen?', suggested more time and doing more of the same would be sufficient for Stuart to achieve his goals. There has been change and it is relevant to the client and salient to his problem. A therapist may be so used to working in a problem focused frame with a 'depth' model of psychology that any idea that the client would have enough flexibility and resourcefulness to resolve issues in such a short period can produce a high degree of trepidation and anxiety in the therapist. In short, therapists may not be used to trusting the patient to tackle these issues.

In Solution Focused Therapy, we are prepared to suspend any such assumptions about 'deeper causes' and reasons why the client 'can't get better that quickly', preferring instead to give them a chance if they think that they have good reason to be confident about their ability to manage without us.

The rule of 'Ockham's Razor' suggests, 'What could be done with fewer means is done in vain with many' (William of Ockham, fourteenth century philosopher cited in Urmson and Rée (1991)). In other words, keeping out of the client's way if they have ethical, moral and legal ways of resolving the problem is the simplest basis on which to proceed. Later, it may be that their solution didn't work out and other factors may come to light to explain this, but proceeding in this way ensures we move at the client's pace. The message, since the previous intervention worked, follows the rule of thumb, 'If it works do more of it'.

TH: 'I'm really struck, Stuart, with the changes that you've been making. They took hard work and courage and it's great to hear that they've been paying off with more relaxing times for yourself and your family. It sounds like you've learned a lot about what you are capable of. It sounds like you know what it is that you've been doing that's working and, also, importantly, what you need to do to keep these changes happening. You said you need to stay with the panics rather than avoid them and that involves going out more, going shopping and you also want to continue talking with your wife and spending time with your children.' (Compliments/Acknowledging and Validating). 'Because you believe that you now have the right formula to get you to where you want to be and that you can get there by using what you've learned about yourself, and you don't need to see us any more . . .' (Bridging Statement), 'we'd like to suggest that you continue to notice everything that you do that helps you to stay on track. We wish you all the best.' (Task)

If no change has occurred

If no change has occurred or the change that has occurred is considered to be insufficient, we would attempt to help the client to generate alternative thoughts/behaviours/strategies that they may not have considered, in order that they can break the unhelpful cycle they are in and develop a different pattern of thinking or behaving that may produce the possibility of a solution.

Case example 1

Session 1

Marie is a 26-year-old who is unemployed and has been suffering from depression for the last two years. She has been receiving medication from her GP with no obvious benefit. She was referred by a psychiatrist when she had reported to the GP that her depression was 'getting worse'.

In the first session Marie explained that she would know that she is 'better' (the Miracle Question) when she was going out more, smiling more, and feeling confident about going out on her own sometimes. She would be taking pride in her appearance by holding her head up and talking more when she is in company and by staying in company at the end of the evening, rather than making excuses to go home. In answer to exception questions she explained that she only really felt relaxed when she is with her sister or with her friend she has known since school. On the scaling question, 'Where are you now?', Marie said she was on 1 because she could make herself go out, when necessary, e.g., to go shopping. On the scale, 'How motivated are you?', she replied that she was at 8.

The therapist's message at the end of the first session was:

TH: 'Thank you for coming to talk today. I appreciate that it is not always easy to talk about problems in this sort of setting. By doing so, you have helped me to begin to understand how things are for you. I've heard from you today how tough your life feels for you at the moment and how frustrated you are at not yet finding a way to turn this around. I was very impressed with your ideas that trying to go out to social situations, even when you don't want to do it, might be helpful to you' (Acknowledging and Validating). 'Because you said that making yourself leave your home and spend time with other people or doing things alone has the potential to be better for you than staying at home, and, because you were at 8 on wanting to do something to sort this out . . .' (Bridging Statement), 'I would like to suggest that between now and the next time we meet, you notice everything that you do that you think will be helpful and notice it in such a way that you can tell me about it next time.' (Task)

Session 2

TH: 'What's better?' (Elicit)
CL: 'Nothing, I've been going out more, mixing more, doing what we said and it's still the same.'

TH: 'So, you really tried and it didn't work the way you wanted it to. That must be frustrating for you?'

CL: 'Yes it is, I'm really fed up with all this.'

TH: 'OK, Marie. Well, we met last Tuesday, that's six days ago, when you went away from here, what was the rest of Tuesday like?'

CL: 'Straight after I felt quite hopeful that doing these things would work. I went straight from here to my sister's instead of going home and that always takes my mind off things. When I left there I thought, I'm not going home coz that's what I always do, so I made myself go to the cinema with my friend but I came back and felt as depressed as I always do.'

TH: 'So this didn't work in the way you wanted it to, but, I'm curious, how did you get yourself to break the pattern and try staying out rather than going home? Even though it didn't work, how did you do that?' (Eliciting change *and* Amplifying an exception to Marie's usual behaviour, but at this stage she doesn't see this change as relevant to her goal.)

CL: 'Well, after talking, I realized that if I just went home again that isn't going to help. I'm not going to change my life by staying indoors and I decided to do something else, but I don't know why I bothered.'

TH: 'That sounds like it was hard work. Did you think that this would work straight away or is it something you might have to carry on doing before you notice a change?' (This introduces the idea that change may be hard won and take time, rather than be immediate.)

CL: 'Well, I thought that going out would make me feel better but apart from taking my mind off things, this didn't make a difference.'

TH: 'So, was there anything else that was different about Tuesday?'

CL: 'No, not really.'

TH: 'OK what's different about Wednesday?'

CL: 'Nothing much. I didn't really do anything on Wednesday apart from stay in bed and watch TV.'

TH: 'Are you sure, Marie, that even though you didn't go out there wasn't something different about Wednesday?'

CL: 'No, I can't think of anything.'

TH: 'What about Thursday? What was Thursday like?' (Marie could not identify anything different about the rest of the week until Sunday. The therapist continued throughout to Elicit, Amplify and Start Again.)

TH: 'What about Sunday?'

CL: 'Well, I went out, I phoned my friend and we went out in the early afternoon and I stayed out till late evening.'

TH: 'Is that different for you, to stay out?'

CL: 'Yeah, I normally make some excuse to come home earlier than that.'

TH: 'So, what was different on this occasion?'

CL: 'I guess I was having fun. We went round the shops in the afternoon and then for a drink and then my friend suggested we go to a club.'

TH: 'And you did?'

CL: 'Yes, it was OK. I had a couple of drinks, was talking a lot and the music was good, it was nice. I even had a dance.'

TH: 'Really? Did this just come naturally or did you have to push yourself to do this?'

CL: 'I didn't really think about it while I was there but I can't do this every night and when I got back it was the same. I think things will always be like this.'

Although Marie has been doing things she felt would help and, to some extent helped while she was doing them, she doesn't see them as relevant or effective in dealing with her overall goal of feeling more confident and lifting her depression. The process of asking questions that identify change, risk taking and hard work, can be useful in gradually helping clients to see themselves as trying hard, making change (no matter how small) and being resourceful even if this may not occur during the interview itself.

It is important that the therapist accepts the client's view of things and doesn't attempt to force or persuade her into seeing changes as being beneficial before the client is ready to see them that way. Eliciting change is not about wearing rose-coloured spectacles. The therapist remains curious and flags changes (e.g., saying 'really') when the client discloses change, but overall matches the client's pace and emotional tone. Relevant exceptions can only be 'built' if the client 'builds with you'.

Because Marie said that these changes were not helping her, it would be useful for the therapist to find out what change would be relevant to her. In the solution focused 'experiment' to discover what helps (tasks) we have found out what hasn't worked at this time, so we move on to help the client explore what further possibilities she feels may be effective.

TH: 'So these things haven't helped you in the way you hoped they would. What do you think would really have made a difference when you came home on Sunday night, for things to have really been different?'

CL: 'I suppose if I had a reason to get up in the mornings.'

TH: 'What would be a good enough reason?'

CL: 'I don't know, having somewhere to go . . . a job . . . someone to get up for.'

TH: 'Someone to get up for?'

CL: 'A boyfriend. In a way it's more lonely coming back from a club.'

TH: 'So you really miss having someone special in your life? That's what you really want?'

CL: 'Yeah.'

TH: 'So, out of the job, being busy, having a boyfriend, which would be most useful to work on now?'

CL: 'I think having a boyfriend is really important for me at the moment.'

The therapist now has a new goal and, so, can reformulate small steps towards this new goal using scales, exceptions and solution focused messages. The therapist interviews in such a way that helps Marie re-define what she wants from her therapy. Her original goals in session one were to go out more and work on 'self confidence'. Through taking this path as an experiment she has learned that what is most important to her is not mere social activity, but a meaningful relationship. Marie's new goal (a relationship) makes further activity meaningful to her.

Therapists new to this approach can, often, be discouraged by 'no change' answers in the EARS section of the interview. However, this example illustrates how a client's goals can change between sessions and how even a 'no change' scenario can help a client clarify what they really want. In our experience, a client's goals will be modified by the interviewing process from session to session.

Change of the right kind (but insufficient)

If the client describes changes that have occurred between the first and present session, and they consider them to be helpful but insufficient, the therapist will, then, interview in an attempt to discover from the client what else it is that they need to do. Possibilities include 'Do more of what's already working', introducing 'time frames', since some changes cannot occur immediately, and 'What else needs to be happening that isn't?'.

Case example 2

Session 1

Bill, aged 54, attended for the first session, having been sent from his GP with a diagnosis of 'work-related stress disorder'. He was a highly successful personnel manager, known for his 'incisive mind' and 'troubleshooting', but recently he said he had been avoiding all decisions at work. This was being noticed by those around him who, usually, passed on their problems to him to solve. His 'miracle' saw him calmer at home with more time for himself and his wife. He was not sure if he wanted in his 'miracle' to solve everyone else's problems as he had done, but work colleagues would see him looking more relaxed by smiling more, speaking up more in meetings and clearing his in-tray. There were clear exceptions, times when he felt better about himself and more decisive. They coincided with weekends, Fridays, and when he took exercise and went jogging, which also helped him to sleep. He was 10 on his 'willingness to do' scale and 3 on his 'where are you now?' scale. He was not very confident at this stage, he could solve things only on 2 on a 'how confident are you scale?'. The message was:

TH: 'I'm impressed with how much thought you have given this situation. It seems you really want your life to change and are attempting to put yourself and your family first and you say this is new for you. We are impressed with what you are already doing, jogging, focusing on weekends, trying to relax, etc.' (Compliments/Validation). 'Because you have said these things are beginning to make a difference but you are not sure how much I'd like to suggest . . .' (Bridging Statement), 'you notice how you continue to do what you are already finding helpful and anything else that makes you feel a little more confident that you can solve this problem.' (Task)

Session 2

TH: 'So, what's better?' (Elicit)
CL: 'Things have been just a little better. I've carried on jogging and I've been sleeping a little better than of late.'
TH: 'Really? So how has this helped you, Bill?' (Amplifying)
CL: 'Well, I suppose jogging helps me switch off, feel physically tired and that I'm looking after myself.'
TH: 'So, you have been jogging and sleeping better?' (Re-stating). 'What has your wife noticed that's a bit better as a result of this?' (Starting again to elicit, using a relationship question.)

CL: 'She said I'm smiling a little more and don't shout at breakfast so much.'

TH: 'So, what has she noticed you doing instead of shouting?' (Amplifying and changing an absence of something to the presence of something new.)

CL: 'Talking to her more, asking about what she'll be doing today, that sort of thing.'

TH: 'So, what difference has this made to her?'

CL: 'I suppose she's a bit more talkative, not so worried about me.'

TH: 'What else?' (Start again)

CL: 'Nothing really.'

TH: 'What about your colleagues at work, Bill? What have they noticed that's different about you?'

CL: 'Well, they wouldn't notice anything. I'm still not "there" at work. The in-tray gets bigger and bigger and nothing's got any better there.'

TH: 'So, anything else that's just a little better?'

CL: 'Nope.'

TH: 'So, remember that scaling question from last session when I asked you where you were on a scale of 0 to 10, with 0 being this problem at its worst and 10 being where you want your life to be. Where would you say you are today?'

CL: 'Err, 4.'

TH: 'So, tell me again, Bill, how have you moved to 4?'

CL: 'Well, the jogging, I know that helped and I'm getting on better with my wife and I've got a holiday coming up in two weeks, I'm looking forward to that.'

TH: 'How will the holiday help?'

CL: 'It will get me away from work for two weeks.'

TH: 'So, what difference will that make to you?'

CL: 'Well, I'm still not coping with it, so at least I won't have to worry about it.'

TH: 'So, things are still really tough for you at work?'

CL: 'Yes, things are tough.'

TH: 'So, you said you are on a 4 on the scale. What would need to happen for you to get to 5?'

CL: 'Well, I don't think anything can be better unless I do something about work, at the moment I'm just running away from it.'

There has been change (jogging, relationship improvements, smiling, etc.). It is the kind of change the client is aiming at and has come to light as a result of the elicit, amplify, reinforce, start again questioning sequence. However, the change, although of the right sort, is not enough. The therapist, therefore, engages in the second stage which is,

'What else needs to happen for progress to be maintained?'. In Bill's case this elicits the fact that he does not believe progress can be achieved unless he deals with his work situation. The therapist's task now is to find out what Bill needs to do in order for him to feel that he is addressing this facet of his difficulty.

TH: 'What would tell you that you are beginning to handle work just that little bit better?'

CL: 'I'd be making decisions again. I used to be very decisive, trouble-shooting, perhaps too much, nothing bothered me. I was really interested in the technicalities at one time.'

TH: 'Technicalities of?'

CL: 'I used to write papers and people would bring me complex documents to amend and I liked that rather than the mundane stuff I do now.'

TH: 'So, while you are waiting for your consultancy business to develop, what will you have to do to resolve the situation at work?'

CL: 'I suppose I should try to take on jobs that interest me, not just solve problems for the others in the office who are not pulling their weight and couldn't care less.'

TH: 'On a scale of 0 to 10, how confident are you now that you can do this?'

CL: 'Well, I didn't really realise 'till I spoke to you how definite I was about working for myself, so I think I can begin to be more selective and say no more often.'

TH: 'Really? So how confident on this scale?'

CL: '8.'

TH: 'So, this goal of working for yourself is very important to you and you realize that you have to take care of yourself at your day job.'

CL: 'That's right, because if I don't keep my head together I'll never get my own business up and running.'

TH: 'What else do you need to do?'

CL: 'I need to start looking after myself more at home. I'm going to keep weekends as my time or else I'll wear out. Make use of holidays to rest up, etc.'

The therapist goes on to develop small behavioural descriptions of how Bill can take care of himself and follow his goal. From a situation where the therapist was simply asking, 'What else needs to happen?', the client began to see himself as 'bored' rather than 'indecisive' and as making a career decision, rather than being 'ill'. The therapist, carefully, ensured the client was not taking on too much and, ironically, his vision of self employment led to him deciding to look after himself more, spend more time with his wife and changing his attitude to work.

Change does not happen in isolation and there are always consequences to any change. Therefore, it is important that the therapist helps the client to address these consequences. In Bill's case, this involved encouraging him to look at how working towards his goals could affect his marriage. The end of session message included the task to, 'Notice how you begin to introduce these ideas of looking after yourself at work, and looking after your marriage at home'.

Paradoxically, the idea of Bill taking on his own company as a second job had the effect of motivating him to manage his work time better, keep his weekends and holidays for his family and relax more. From an 'expert' position it would have been hard to imagine.

TH: 'So, how could you get a bit of that interest back?'
CL: 'Actually, I'm beginning to wonder myself whether it is possible. My job has changed so much. I think I could get it away from work.'
TH: 'Tell me more.'
CL: 'Well, I've started up a small consultancy company and I deal with technical stuff and it's great.'
TH: 'Really, hold on, one of the things you said was that you needed more time for yourself, so how does more work help?'

The therapist is willing to accept the client's solution to his 'mundane' job up to the point where it becomes uncertain whether the new solution (more work) is helpful or, in fact, adds to his stress. This dilemma is made overt and put back to the client so that he can clarify what's happening.

CL: 'Actually, it really helps a lot because I'm beginning to wonder how come I can be decisive in my own company and not at work.'
TH: 'That's a good question, Bill. What do you think?'
CL: 'Maybe I've just lost interest and motivation because I'm bored and need a challenge.'
TH: 'So, what do you know about yourself that tells you can manage these two jobs?' (Bill still has not explained to us whether this would be an added burden or an asset.)
CL: 'I've always thrived on a challenge, I treat it like a hobby. I see my consultancy work becoming my full-time job in the future. My wife thinks it's a good idea, she doesn't want me working for the day job, anyway.'

TH: 'How confident is your wife that you will manage this transition?'
CL: 'Well, we have talked about this a lot because she was worried I might be taking on too much and we would drift apart, but she says that she thinks it's the right move for me and the other company is dragging me down. She wants me to keep her involved in what I am doing.'
TH: 'So, what will you and your wife have to do to look after each other while you are doing this?'
CL: 'Talk. Keep time for each other. Have fun on holiday.'

This is possible and we may have prescribed anything but extra work. This is an interesting example of the client, undoubtedly, knowing best. If you are able to cooperate with the client's goals (in this case Bill's consideration for his wife and plan to stop himself from burning out, allowed us to cooperate with his goal of his own company) they will, often, lead you to an elegant solution by a surprising route, in some cases a route that other therapies would close off.

8

Complainant, visitor and customer relationships

Learning objectives

Three concepts are introduced that help the therapist keep track of which kind of relationship they have at any one time with a client. Readers will be able to differentiate between these and be aware of methods that may move the therapist/client relationship to be as productive as soon as possible.

For simplicity's sake, the Brief Family Therapy Centre, characterized three types of relationship: 'complainant'; 'visitor'; and 'customer'. These terms are used to help identify the nature of the therapeutic relationship at any one time. They are not labels to be used to identify particular types of *client*, but refer loosely to the *relationship*. It is possible to move between all three in the process of a single session. These concepts help therapists to identify what kind of conversation to engage in so they can be most helpful and how to pace the sessions at the client's speed. They also stop therapists from 'racing ahead', trying to develop goals for the person in front of them when the person in front of them may not want to be there at all or may want someone else to change to resolve the situation.

The therapist and client engage in what is intended to be a mutually collaborative relationship. The nature of this collaboration is defined by the goals that the client has at any particular time.

Complainant

In a complainant relationship, the client attends primarily to 'get something off their chest'. They feel that the problem lies with someone or something else, e.g., 'My husband/wife/boss really needs to change before I can feel any better'. They might have some idea (realistic or unrealistic) that this problem can be changed but are not sure that it is within their control.

As a rule of thumb with complainant relationships questions such as, 'How realistic is it that you could change your partner/boss/ teacher?' should be asked. The therapist may offer to see the other person only if the other person feels it might help. While you try to cooperate, it is important that you do not take responsibility on behalf of the client for changing a third party. For example:

CL: 'Will you see my daughter and make her see sense?'
TH: 'How likely is it that she would respond to something you or I may say to her in a session like this?'

Sometimes clients request very simple and straightforward actions from therapists such as, 'Will you let my GP know that I did come and what I said?' or 'Can we not meet together as a family with the social worker and teachers there to explain things?', and we would not dismiss such requests out of hand (remember, a simple solution is often all that is needed). It is still important that the client thinks this through with the therapist so that they have a clear idea of how doing this would help. The therapist has to have a clear idea of what the client wants them to do so that they can decide whether they can or should comply.

If a goal is unrealistic the 'non-miracle' scenario, as described earlier in the chapter, is used to try to identify a goal for the client *themselves*. So lots of questions such as, 'While you are waiting to leave school what would help you cope with it a little better?', may be appropriate. The therapist proceeds on a logical basis in order to clarify what influence anyone might have over the situation, and to check if the client themselves has some influence which they may have overlooked.

There are three possible outcomes to this questioning routine:

1. The client establishes that they can do something to influence the situation.
2. The client establishes that someone else is able and willing to influence the situation.
3. The client establishes in their own mind that nothing is likely to influence the situation.

The kinds of questions that can be used with a complainant relationship include:

'What are the chances that you will be able to change this situation?'
'Are you sure that you are unable to influence this situation even in some small way?'
'Who is the person most likely to be able to change your (husband/ wife/ boss, etc.)?'
'Can you see yourself at some point in the future being able to change your . . . ?'
'What needs to happen before you can get to that stage?'
'Who or what can help you achieve this change?'
'Do you know of anyone (friends/family, etc.) who have had a similar problem and have sorted it out?' (If yes, 'How did they do it?')
'Have you had a problem similar to this in the past that you have handled successfully?'
'Do you think there might be something that we haven't considered that might help the situation?'

These are all questions that could be seen as designed to loosen the clients' 'fixed frame' and generate doubt or curiosity about their level of influence.

Scaling questions are also useful as part of this process. For example, 'On a scale of 0 to 10, where 10 is that you are certain that your boss can change and 0 is that there isn't a snowball's chance in hell, what are the chances on a scale of 0 to 10?'.

If these questions generate ideas, curiosities, hopes or alternative actions, that the client could develop to change the other person, it is now possible to proceed with the client taking an active part in attaining this goal of changing the other person; a goal that the client now feels is possibly under their control. 'What would be the next step that would see you move up one scale' can then be used and you have moved into a customer relationship.

If after these questions the client still believes the other person is not likely to change, then this in itself is a useful marker to help the client think the situation through further: 'Given the fact that on a scale of 0 to 10, you think there is 0 chance your boss will change, what can you do to make your life a little bit better?' Through using these questions you may help to establish a fresh, alternative goal which is not about their boss but is about the client changing *themselves* or coping better with the situation.

Case example

Lillian, aged 56, attended following a referral by her doctor for 'depression and anxiety'. Her answer to the Miracle Question was that her husband would change. For the whole of their marriage she felt that they had not even got to know each other and that he did his thing and expected her to stay at home and provide for him. She felt this was a role that she had been 'trained for' by 'her generation' but was unhappy at present with her eldest son's marriage and her husband's refusal to go. Questions such as, 'What are the chances you can change your husband between 0 to 10, where 0 is that you have no chance and 10 is that it would be very easy, where would you be?', produced minus scores. Lillian was absolutely sure he wouldn't change now and that he wouldn't come to therapy with or without her. 'While you are waiting for something to change your husband, what could you do to make things a little more bearable?', led to ideas about going out more and joining an art class, since Lillian was good at art but had never had the encouragement to take part. This new goal of discovery for herself led to a customer relationship.

If the client or therapist think that counselling has no part to play in helping to change a system or person then the client is again 'let go', with the offer of further contact when something changes that means counselling could help.

Visitor

In a visitor relationship, the client attends primarily because they have been sent, or advised to come by somebody else, or are required to attend as part of a statutory arrangement (e.g., probation setting). Typical responses to, 'What brought you here?' include 'My doctor/ social worker, probation officer, boss sent me'. To further establish the basis that the client attended you can follow up with, 'Do you agree that you need to come?'. If the client does agree that they need to see you they are in a customer relationship. If not then you have a visitor-type relationship with them, at least for the moment.

In a visitor situation, the therapist is open, positive and respectful and interviews to discover if there is anything that the client would like to talk about that would be interesting for them. Goals from the client (such as, 'I'd like to convince my teacher that I don't need counselling', or 'I'd like to get my mum off my back') can be explored using questions like: 'How will that help you?'; 'What chances have you got of persuading them?'; 'What would be the smallest thing that you could do that might change their mind about you having to come here?'; or 'What kind of changes would they need to see to stop pressurizing you to come here?', etc. Once again, by initially cooperating with such 'negative' goals, alternative behaviours that may help the client, be interesting to them and effect change (acceptable to the client and the person that has sent them) may be identified. Goals such as, 'I'd like you to give me a lot of money so that I can get drunk' are 'laughed off' as impossible and followed by the questions 'How would that help?' or 'What else could we do that might be helpful?'.

If the client still presents a genuine dilemma, for example, 'My consultant psychiatrist says I have to attend regularly or he'll need to admit me, but coming here winds me up so much that it makes things worse', it is important for the therapist to stay neutral in the situation, asking the questions without blaming either party. He should respond with responses such as 'This sounds like a tough situation. How are you going to sort this out?' which place responsibility on the client without being disrespectful to the client or the other professionals involved. This is 'just the way it is' and should be treated as a logical dilemma.

On occasion, if the therapist is warm and respectful and is willing to listen, the client may present some other problem that they do feel able to change and would like to work on (see the 'Girl who wanted to make friends' Chapter 7 case study 1 'Marie', pp. 69–72). Working on any goal that the client is willing to focus on may eventually impinge on the area of difficulty for which they were originally sent.

If the relationship does not evolve through the questions into a customer relationship, the therapist needs to consider, 'Have I a statutory or legal responsibility to this case?'. If the answer is yes, then the therapist is in the realms of management rather than therapy and will maintain regular contact in order to fulfil their role to their agency's satisfaction, re-asking the solution focused questions from time to time to try and engage the client in a productive piece of work. If there is no legal or statutory responsibility and no agency requirement to see the client, the therapist will double check that there is really nothing they can do for the client and then let them go since there is no contract for therapy.

Visitor relationship where an alternative goal emerges

Stephanie, aged 26, was brought along to a session by her parents who did not want to sit in themselves. She had been 'drinking excessively' and cutting her arms as well as eating little and vomiting. Her parents were understandably worried and had expressed this to their GP, who put in the referral letter, but on talking to Stephanie initially she denied that eating or drinking was a problem. She did respond to the Miracle Question and described a scenario in which she was able to make more friends. Part of this miracle, where she had more friends and went out more, turned out to be that she would be drinking less and be 'more in control' with no cutting, since her friends disapproved of her drunken and unpredictable behaviour. In subsequent sessions she also, eventually, approached the issue of changing her eating habits when it seemed that she began to trust the therapist.

Because the therapist did not insist on her parents' agenda (one which she, initially, disagreed with) the relationship changed from a reluctant client to one in which Stephanie had her own goals. As a result of focusing on these, the parents' concerns were also addressed.

Visitor relationship where there are no alternative goals

Robert, a 50-year-old police officer, was referred by his GP with a diagnosis of 'personality disorder'. The referral letter contained information about recent visits to the surgery when Robert had become verbally aggressive, shouted at receptionist staff and had been 'difficult' with both the GP and the practice counsellor. The therapist began the session with the alternative question 'What would have to happen for today to be a success?', and Robert immediately responded with 'You would give me a sickness certificate'. He described his firm belief that he should not have to return to work and was disillusioned by recent changes in early retirement financial packages given to police officers. He had expected to be in a better financial position and to have been supported on sickness benefits from work for much longer, and 'retired'. This had not happened and he had to see his GP in order to continue to receive an income. The GP he felt, in order to 'help', was sending him to lots of different therapists and he was adamant he had no problem other than frustration and low finances.

The therapist asked the Miracle, relationship and exception questions, and Robert's responses were consistent with his idea there was no problem other than money. The therapist asked if there was anything at all that he could help him with and mentioned that there was something about 'panic attacks' in his referral letter and he stated he did not have these but had discussed them with the personnel department to see if they would help his goal of retirement. He declined any help and the intervention was one of thanking him for coming along, commenting on his frustration, respecting his wishes and agreeing to write to his GP, stating that he had attended. Robert was discharged and stated he was happy with the session and if he ever did have a problem he felt counselling could help, he would contact us again.

In our opinion, professionals often get 'stuck' with cases when their enthusiasm or conscientiousness drives them to take responsibility for helping clients who have no realistic goal for themselves within the context of therapy. It is, we feel, more respectful to let clients go with the offer that if they feel we could help with anything in the future, they can contact us.

Customer relationships

Customer relationships are the most straightforward. The client has a problem they want to work on with the therapist, actively seek the therapeutic process and feel able to influence their situation to bring about change for themselves.

Final case example

To illustrate that it is possible to pass through all three stages, Samantha was referred by her GP for 'psychotherapy' as he felt that she needed to grieve for her recently dead husband. She had suicidal thoughts and was now on antidepressant medication. Samantha did not agree with her GP, did not want to be there to work on grief at all, but did respond to the more 'open', early questions. Her answer to the Miracle Question revolved around her cementing her relationship with her newly found partner whose behaviour towards her was unpredictable in that he would arrive unexpectedly and leave on impulse. She felt she would like the relationship to be more stable and was intrigued by whether this was possible.

When asked the exception questions, she responded by saying that if she didn't pressure her partner over meals, didn't call every day and went somewhere on her own, he was more interested and considerate. The therapist has some assumptions (that the relationship was not a promising one as Samantha seemed to be treated inconsiderately, and was unable to assert herself) which were suspended in favour of asking about what she wanted for herself and the steps needed to achieve this.

Samantha began to put ideas of going out more, meeting her friends, not calling every day and not always preparing meals into practice. She reported that, as a result of this, she felt 'better in herself' and her self-esteem improved. Much to her surprise (she previously felt such a course of action impossible) she found herself becoming appropriately angry and assertive when she felt she was being treated badly. Not only did the relationship survive this (she had an idea if she asserted herself her partner would leave) but over five sessions she reported change in her partner and more commitment shown by a move to buy a house together.

Interestingly, when the stability of the relationship ceased to be such a predominant issue for Samantha, she then began to work through some of the feeling about her husband dying suddenly. She felt, after six sessions, that the situation had improved to such an extent she could leave therapy and stop her antidepressant medication, with her GP's permission.

Samantha moved through visitor, complainant and customer relationships during the course of the therapy. Initially, we had a visitor relationship in terms of the original referral and the client was not willing to cooperate with an agenda around grief. She wanted her partner to change in order to improve her life and felt, initially, she had no control over this (complainant relationship), but the exception questions highlighted the fact that she did have some influence on the situation and a customer relationship was then possible. As a 'side effect' of solution focused questioning, she also began to assert herself with her partner in a way that she did not previously think possible, and began to deal with her feeling of bereavement in a way that concurred with the GP's original referral. She tackled things in the order she felt was appropriate, rather than the order the professionals (including us) may have wanted.

The therapist, in this case, was tempted to address gender issues and power in relationships whenever this was addressed. Samantha, clearly, stated this was not how she saw things and that her 'sister has already told me to stand up for myself and finish with him, it didn't help then and it's not what I want now'. Since there were no safety issues or marital violence to consider, the therapist suspended these ideas and Samantha solved these issues through own goals and her own route.

Summary

We have described three types of relationship within therapy and the kind of questioning that needs to happen so that the therapist can help the client to consider options available. Some of them may result in continued contact and, occasionally, it becomes clear that therapy can be terminated. If the therapist works in an inpatient hospital setting or has a statutory or managerial role, then contact is continued but on the basis of management or monitoring the client. Solution focused questions can still be used from time to time to assess the basis for any continuing therapeutic work.

9

Working with 'psychosis'

Learning objectives

This chapter explores the application of Solution Focused Therapy with clients who have a diagnosis of 'psychosis'. By the end of the chapter, the reader will understand the idea of psychotic ideas as a 'means to an end', the logical nature of the approach, the differing roles of 'manager' and 'therapist' and the implications of cooperating with the client's goals. Case material from the authors and de Shazer's comments on the issue are included.

Rules of thumb regarding 'psychosis'

1. Suspend your assumptions about the label or diagnosis.
2. Talk to the client as a person, not as a label.
3. Accept that their opinion about their problem is as valid as anyone else's.
4. Complicated problems do not, necessarily, require complicated solutions.
5. Accept that the client's goals may not fit in with yours.
6. Listen to what the client says they want.
7. Bizarre or unrealistic responses to the Miracle Question are acceptable as a starting place in therapy.
8. The use or non-use of medication by the client is not an issue in the selection of 'suitable' clients or a measure for success.

9. Statutory responsibilities override therapy. If the client is considered a danger to themselves or others, management's and their safety becomes your primary responsibility.
10. Don't panic.

How should we read 'psychosis'?

First, some clients with this diagnosis will be unable to engage in a conversation with a therapist at all. At workshops, a common statement is, 'The clients we see on the wards are too high to benefit from counselling'. It may be necessary for clients to be 'stabilized' to a level at which they can sit for a period of time with the therapist and talk about the issues. No model of therapy is effective if clients cannot stay in the same room as the therapist and converse occasionally. As this is our only exception of a client, it allows us to have a broad referral criteria.

Many counsellors and carers work, extensively, with a wide client group and never meet a client with a diagnosis of 'psychosis', 'manic depressive psychosis', 'schizophrenia' or 'schizo-affective disorder'. It has taken us fifteen years to realize that we don't know what the words mean. Hopefully, the earlier chapters have gone some way towards releasing us from negative assumptions about any diagnostic label. Diagnosis, on its own, does not tell us enough about the client. We need to have a conversation with them. These conditions are said to be characterized by (and their symptoms learned by rote of countless nurses, psychiatrists, medics, etc.) lack of insight which may be accompanied by delusion material, hallucinations, ideas of reference, thought disturbance, etc.

Psychological therapies that require the client to have a degree of insight and motivation would regard clients with a history of 'psychosis' as unsuitable. For example, Yallom (1931) developed criteria that assessed the suitability of people for psychodynamic group therapy. Suitable clients should be:

young;
attractive;
verbal;
intelligent;
successful.

With some exceptions, psychoanalytic psychotherapy would be extremely wary of engaging in therapy with psychotic clients as they would be regarded as being liable to get worse because of the process of psychodynamic work.

Traditionally, treatment for such difficulties consisted of medication, management and 'reality reinforcement', e.g., 'I understand that you can hear voices at the moment, but I can't hear them'. Little else was on offer. More recently, the idea has developed that this attitude is unfair to people who have a right to engage in therapeutic conversations, regardless of how 'successful' the therapist believes they can be. The recent challenge to helping professionals has been the need for statutory services to provide more for the 'seriously, mentally ill': 'There is, now, evidence to suggest that psychological techniques may provide an alternative in the treatment of people with psychotic disorders' (Bradshaw and Haddock, 1995).

Not all therapists followed the assumption that this client group is 'untreatable' through therapeutic conversations. Milton Erickson saw 'schizophrenics' as 'living a metaphoric life' which is an idea strangely free of the negative inferences the diagnosis can evoke in us. He believed that it was helpful to work within the client's world view, rather than to oppose it with reality reinforcement.

Erickson (in Haley, 1973) assumes that with a schizophrenic, the important message is the metaphor. For example, when Erickson was on the staff of Worcester State Hospital, there was a young patient who called himself Jesus. He paraded about as the Messiah, wore a sheet draped around him and attempted to impose Christianity on people. Erickson approached him in the hospital grounds and said 'I understand you have experience as a carpenter?'. The patient could only reply that he had. Erickson involved the young man in a special project of building a book case and shifted him to productive labour.

Ben Furman and Tapani Ahola state that:

> Sometimes clients' own explanations for their problems may appear inappropriate to professionals. In such cases, therapists often try to persuade the client to adopt another explanation. For example, if the parents of a boy presume that his behavioural problems are caused by the fact that he struck his head as an infant, the therapist may wish the parents to adopt another explanation in order for them to become empowered to solve the problem.
>
> Sometimes when clients are convinced beyond doubt of the correctness of their own explanation, it may prove futile to try and persuade them otherwise. In such situations the therapist may choose to subscribe to the principle of 'don't argue with the client' and accept the client's explanation at face value.
>
> (Furman and Ahola, 1992, p. 87)

Solution Therapy is concerned with what the client wants to do differently to make their life better, rather than imposing a certain view of 'reality' on an individual.

Once we embrace this concept it matters little whether the parents in Ben Furman's example believe the cause of their son's behaviour was a fall or a result of 'bad parenting', what matters is that their son's behaviour changes. In this case, the parents are more likely to join with the therapist in changing things if they are allowed to keep their beliefs about cause. Once again, what happened to cause an event is of less significance in this model than what the client wants to do to make things better.

Accepting a client's world view does not mean that a Solution Therapist would condone this view as being the most helpful one to hold. We would see it as a means to developing cooperation with the client. De Shazer says that he will accept a client's view up to the point at which it becomes unhelpful, unethical or dangerous to continue to do so. At this point, we may once again be in the realms of management of a client for their own protection or society's, rather than therapy.

The question with this type of client is not, 'How can we persuade the client that the voices are inside his head?' but 'What does the client want to do to control, minimize and eradicate them and how can we help them in this?', and 'What do we have to do to ensure their safety at this time?'. This willingness to respect the client's explanation of the cause or perception of a problem allows us to engage their curiosity and cooperation in finding a solution to it. Furman and Ahola (1992) go on to say, 'Explanations can be examined not in terms of whether they are correct or not, but in terms of what actions they invoke' (p. 90).

Technique

Initially the Solution Focused therapist interviews using the same techniques as we would use for any interview. The structure of the sessions is the same. However, if the client responds to the 'What brought you here?' or 'How can we help?' question with 'delusional' material we remain curious about:

1. how the client knows what they think they know;
2. how they think that somebody else would deal with a similar problem;
3. whether they are sure that this is the only explanation;
4. what their family, friends, etc., think about this;
5. is there anyone that disagrees with them about this? How come?

Initially, therefore, we interview to map the 'outline' of the client's world view and to assess the flexibility of their beliefs. If their beliefs appear unshakeable we attempt to 'deconstruct' them, challenging with logic. We use the term 'deconstruction' in the same way as Goolishian who defined it thus: 'To deconstruct means to take apart the interpretative assumptions of the system of meaning that you are examining, to challenge the interpretative system in such a manner that you reveal the assumptions on which the model is based. At the same time as these are revealed, you open the space for alternative understanding' (Anderson and Goolishian, 1989, p. 11).

If the system is still unshakeable we 'agree to disagree' and attempt to accept the client's reasons for the problem and explore how the client could cope differently with their life and how they can cope with the situation if they truly take into account the repercussions of their beliefs. In effect we 'disconnect' the explanation from the action the client could take to make life better for themselves: 'OK, if your son is this way because of a fall how can I help?; How would you like him to be different from now on?'

To sum up, we look for areas that ethically we can cooperate with and continue to have a conversation that allows these areas to be expanded. This is in keeping with the solution focused belief that staying 'on the surface' through description and conversation (rather than interpretation or looking behind and beneath what the client says to divine meaning) will provide the information necessary to help the client to move forward.

'Psychotic clients' can be marginalized by society. They are often excluded from therapeutic conversations due to referral criteria and the belief that psychotic content cannot be worked with. When they do have access to therapy it is all too easy to exclude the client even further if the conversation is restricted to separating and constantly challenging the client's psychosis. This suggests that the psychotic material is somehow inappropriate for therapy and the client errant for holding such ideas.

Solution therapy is a model of inclusion, allowing the client to discuss 'psychotic' material without negative comment or value judgement. Therapists include the client by inquiring about 'universal truths' that we all share, e.g., the future goals wishes are plans of how to achieve these goals, etc. The conversation is therefore about the commonality between psychotic clients and the therapist. Given that people are often frightened and isolated by delusional ideas this 'policy' of introducing common ground may allow the client to feel less 'crazy'.

We expand the ideas of existing mental health in the client's wishes, goals, hopes and desire to change. We therefore conduct a conversation about mental health rather than illness, about what is common between people (of any diagnosis) rather than what is different. As with 'visitor relationships', goals such as 'Not having to see you again', 'Being out of hospital', and 'Being off medication' are acceptable starting places and met with: 'OK, what has to happen so that we don't have to meet like this?'; 'What would the doctors, your family or the staff have to see that would lead them to agree with you?'

Solution therapists will focus on any goals or material that reflect areas of mental health or have the potential to lead clients into mental health. For example, goals such as wanting to be calmer, to trust others or to be free of voices that trouble you are valid areas for the therapist to work on with the client. Such work takes the form of 'What helps?'. As with any answer to this question, the therapist expands on any exceptions to the problem that are salient, achievable and ethical.

If a client stated that he wanted to line his room with tinfoil in order to block out radio waves that plague him, we would see this solution as a means to an end: Means = Tinfoil lining; End = Peace and quiet. Peace and quiet is a goal that we can wholeheartedly work on with the client. There will be other means to achieve peace and quiet other than the tinfoil solution. For example: Means could = Tinfoil lining/wearing a helmet/playing your music louder/taking medication as prescribed/learning to ignore such voices/talking to someone/staying with relatives/moving bedrooms, etc.; End = peace and quiet. Obviously some Means in the above list a therapist would be more able ethically to cooperate with than others, but at least there are more choices for the client.

As we will explore in the chapter on suicide, suicidal clients can be described as having a poverty of choice. Their perception of the situation leads to a belief that there is only one solution. Psychosis brings about similar lack of choice and so by identifying the ends and by joining with the client to creatively brainstorm alternative solutions you introduce a wider range of means.

Also, although the means may be illogical, eccentric or crazy (tinfoil, wearing a helmet) the end is often understandable, valid and sane (peace and quiet, sleep). We all want peace and to feel safe, to feel we can trust others, etc. We don't all achieve this by hiding away, wearing a loincloth or lining our rooms with tinfoil. If you look beyond the client's attempted solution the end they desire is often salient, understandable and sane.

In our opinion, most training and theories get stuck in the means part of the equation, exploring unusual ideas and trying to dissuade the client from their point of view.

Case example

Session 1

Bob is a 54-year-old unemployed train driver. He is married with two children aged 16 and 20. He was referred by his Community Psychiatric Nurse for treatment. He had a long-standing belief that the water supply to his house was poisoned, which led over the years to the water board digging up his garden to try and find the fault and to him having the piping replaced in his house, neither of which eradicated the problem for him. He remained convinced that the water was poisoned and he had stopped using it for washing, cooking or drinking. His wife now made daily trips to the supermarket to buy bottled water. No amount of dissuasion from his family (who still used the water) or from professionals could shake him from his belief. Bob and his wife, June, attended the session.

TH: 'What brought you here today?'

June: 'Well, it's really because we are all so worried about Bob. He has had this idea for a long time that all the water in the house is poisoned. I don't know why because myself and the kids continue to use it, but he's convinced and he won't touch it. It's got worse and worse and so the nurse that comes to see him asked us to come and see you.'

TH: 'What have you been doing to handle this so far? What have you tried?'

June: 'Well, he sees the psychiatrist and he's put him on medication, Stelazine.'

TH: 'Has that been helpful?'

Bob: 'Not really, I don't think it's doing anything, and the water IS POISONED. I don't know why they keep saying it's not. I've had the water board out and replaced all the pipes in the house and the water is still funny tasting. I am convinced that it is being poisoned. I don't know why no one will believe me.'

TH: 'So, how are you coping with this?'

Bob: 'Well, I don't drink any of it. I stopped doing that a long time ago. My wife gets the water, bottled water, from town every day and I use that.'

TH: 'What effect does the water have on you?'

Bob: 'It furs up my tongue; tastes foul; I get stomach pains; I'm tired and aching all the time.'

TH: 'How come your family are able to use it?'

Bob: 'I don't know, all I know is that it's poisoned.'

TH: 'What ideas do you have about this, June?'

June: 'Well, we've had all the experts out. We've had all the garden ripped up, the pipes out, no-one's found anything. It tastes OK to me and tastes OK to the kids. We don't seem to suffer by using it. I don't know why he has the idea.'

TH: 'I'm going to ask you both a bit of a strange question. I'll start with you Bob, it takes a bit of imagination. Suppose you go to bed this evening and go to sleep and while you are asleep a miracle happens and the problem that brought you here today is solved, just like that. But you don't know how because you were asleep. When you wake up tomorrow morning what will be the first thing you'll notice that will tell you something is different today, a miracle must have happened in the night?'

Bob: 'Well the water won't be poisoned. It would taste OK.'

TH: 'What difference will that make?'

Bob: 'Well, I guess I'll start drinking tea made with it. And I'll eat food like vegetables again cooked in water. I'll have an ordinary wash again.'

TH: 'What else?'

Bob: 'I suppose it'll make things easier for June, because she won't have to drag round the shops every day for water or cook two dinners for the kids and me because I have to have the stuff separately.'

TH: 'What will she be able to do instead?'

Bob: 'Well, she'll have more time for herself, I think we'll just get on better. I think it will take some of the friction away; we'll probably be happier together.'

TH: 'What will the children see different about you that will tell them a "miracle" has happened?'

Bob: 'They'll see me less grumpy. We'll eat together, I suppose. I'll shout at them less over little things because all this gets you down you know.'

TH: 'What will you be doing with them that you aren't now, that will tell them things are better?'

Bob: 'I don't know, I can't think of anything. They don't notice much now anyway at their age.'

TH: 'So, June, when this "miracle" happens to you and you wake up tomorrow morning and the problem has gone away, what will be different for you?'

June: 'He wouldn't be getting on my nerves, talking about this all the time. Life would be so different. I wouldn't have to make special arrangements for him with the cooking, he'd eat with everybody, he'd just make a cup of tea without a big fuss. We could get back to being normal again and, yes, we would get on better.'

TH: 'OK, so things would be very different but what would be the first thing you would notice?'

June: 'I'd be able to make him a cup of tea without him remarking on it.'

TH: 'That would be different?'

June: 'Yeah.'

TH: 'What would be different about you if this "miracle" happened?'

June: 'I'd have more time. I'd, probably, talk to him more because at the moment I avoid conversations for fear that he'll go on and on about the water again. I'd smile more, we'd have a bit more fun.'

TH: 'What would the kids see different about the pair of you?'

Bob: 'We'd all go out somewhere again, we did used to get on before this water thing happened.'

TH: 'Are there any parts of this miracle happening already?'

June: 'Well, we do get on sometimes, when we watch a film on the TV or something. Obviously, we've stopped going round to friends and family for dinner and things like that.'

TH: 'Are there any times that you manage to drink water, at the moment, in the house from the house pipes?'

Bob: 'No.'

TH: 'But you are still sure that it's poisoned now, even though you've stopped drinking it?'

Bob: 'Well it is, I know it is.'

TH: 'On a scale of 0 to 10, where 0 was this problem at the worst and 10 was the day after the miracle, where would you be now?'

Bob: '0, because nothing's changed about the water.'

June: '4 or 5, because we do get on better, recently, and, at least, I go out to work so it's not 24 hours a day.'

TH: 'On a scale of 0 to 10 where 10 is where you would do anything to solve this problem and 0 where is you can only hope, where are you now?'

June: '10, I want us to be back where we were four years ago.'

Bob: 'Well, I'd like to solve this problem but I don't know what else to do.'

TH: 'Is there anything that you think I missed or wanted to say before I take a break?'

Bob: 'No, I think we've said everything that was important.'

Therapist takes a break.

Message

Well, we would like to thank you both for coming along today. Clearly, it is a serious and worrying problem for you. You have tried a lot to sort it out and it must be frustrating that what you have tried hasn't worked and that it is getting in the way of you having the life that you want together. We loved hearing about you having more time together and smiling more, talking more and being more relaxed with each other and that you can still sit and watch TV and get the occasional break (Compliments, Validation and Acknowledging Strengths). We are really curious about how the family are unaffected and don't understand this, so we will give it more thought, because you really would like to improve things with each other and get back to how you used to be (Bridging Statement). We would like you to notice anything that happens that improves your relationship or changes the difficulty, even in some small way, so that we can talk about it next time (Notice task).

Commentary

Bob arrived with a seemingly fixed idea about the world which seemed relatively immovable. The therapist gently challenged this idea by introducing curiosity and puzzlement at the family's ability to drink water. This is, always, very gentle and its aim is to introduce curiosity and doubt to a fixed system, not to suggest the client is wrong or reinforce reality. Technically, this is deconstruction, using the logical undeniable fact to challenge the system. The water is poisoned but the family can drink it. The challenge is a gentle one, however, and we invite the client to think about this. We would not push this path of questioning to the point where the client has to come up with an answer but only use it to sow the potential seeds of doubt and, therefore, choice.

There were goals outside of the water issue for the couple which were easier to cooperate on. The message, therefore, introduced curiosity about the water situation but was also focused on their goal of getting better. Once again, in Solution Therapy, change is more likely to occur between the sessions rather than during them and if the couple do work on getting on better, the water issue may shift via this path, rather than a head-on assault.

Session 2

Bob and June returned to their second session two weeks later and reported that, although Bob was still refusing to drink household water, there was some improvement in the quality of their relationship.

Bob had suggested going out together and had been helping a little more with the household chores. This had the effect of reducing tension in the family which gave them a respite from their primary concern which remained Bob's conviction that the water was poisoned.

Message

We are impressed that you have taken some steps to care for each other more, recharge your batteries and spend time together. We are still curious about how the family can use domestic water without any ill effect, it puzzles us. Because you have made some positive changes we would like to suggest that you continue with the changes you have started.

Commentary

Even in the second session the therapist still does not know what will emerge as a solution. The temptation is to try and explain why things are happening or dissuade Bob more forcefully. This may give the therapist an illusion of control over the situation creating a sense that the therapist knows what to do to solve this problem, which puts the therapist in an 'expert' role and the client in a passive role. There is no guarantee that the therapist, reacting in the way described, will lead to any solution to the problem and is often adopted to safeguard the therapist's professional self-esteem. The focus is on what helped and small changes which, although outside the area of the complaint, did have some effect on improving the quality of the couple's relationship. There was some change.

Session 3

Bob and June attended for their third session. June reported, with some excitement, that there had been one occasion when Bob, knowingly, ate a meal prepared from the domestic water supply. Bob said he didn't think about it; he gave it no prior thought. He did not notice any ill effects from doing so but was not convinced, himself, about the safety of the water supply and had done this once. In a situation such as this, the therapist paces questions carefully and does not try too hard to get details of how the client made such a change. They, gently, 'flag' the changes with comments such as 'Really?', 'How did you know this was the right thing to do?' but allow the client to remain vague about how the change was achieved. Detail may cause the client to deconstruct their own exception and the purposes for doing so may collapse. If too much is made of an embryonic exception, the client may feel pressed into a 'loose situation'. For example, Bob may begin to feel he was: wrong all these years to believe the water was poisoned; or wrong to eat the food cooked with water that he still believed was poisoned. No one should feel belittled or 'shamefaced' by therapy and to avoid this situation vague exceptions are accepted without any refinement from the therapist.

Session 5

As therapy progressed, the couple elected for longer breaks between appointments. The fifth and final session occurred four months after their initial appointment.

TH: 'So, what's better?'

Bob: 'Well, we just went out for the day, just the two of us and it was really nice. We enjoyed ourselves just walking around and window shopping. We've been getting on better at home just chatting more, she seems to want to be with me more often.'

TH: 'How did you get this to happen?'

Bob: 'I don't know.'

June: 'I do. He's stopped talking about the water all the time and he is washing, eating and drinking with the water from home. He even cooked a meal for us. I'm really surprised. It's made a big difference.'

TH: 'What difference has it made?'

June: 'Well, it's like we're back to normal. I don't have to traipse down the supermarket or carry heavy bottles of water back and we're a lot closer now. We're, actually, having fun more often.'

TH: 'How did you get yourself to do all this?'

Bob: 'I don't know, it just happened. It doesn't seem to be a problem now.'

TH: 'So, you're getting on better, talk together about a wider range of things, going out helps and you are drinking the water again. How are you going to keep these changes happening?'

Bob: 'We've just got to keep making more time for ourselves and try to enjoy life a little more.'

June: 'If he keeps joking like he has been recently, and surprising me with suggestions about days out, then I think that will all help.'

They did not think another appointment was necessary but asked to phone us in the future and attend if they needed to.

Commentary

Change did occur because Bob was not sure how it happened and his wife was happy with the changes. It was important not to press on him the mechanics of change.

Summary

Psychosis can be worked with using Solution Focused Therapy. Our colleagues, working on an acute inpatient unit, used Solution Therapy to assess a young man who was being admitted. His answer to the Miracle Question was, 'My arse would stop melting'. The staff member, simply, continued with the session and was able to explore how the client would know this had happened and what he would be doing differently if this changed. It is a cliché to say that therapeutic engagement with psychotic clients has fallen outside the realm of normal therapeutic process to such an extent that it is taken for granted by most practitioners that any kind of referral for therapeutic work is inappropriate. We have sought to demonstrate by these transcripts, that, while there are undoubted hazards in working therapeutically with other models, a focused approach is not only harmless but can be self-evidently productive.

One of the benefits of this approach is that its concentration on relatively mundane goals tends not to unnerve or over-stimulate the client. The major strands of technique are low-key use of deconstructive initiatives, expressing doubt in a non-threatening way but moving on rather than challenging, directly, ideas which are thought to be delusional. Delusional content is only part of a client's life and in itself may not block the pathway to valuable realistic change.

Exercises

Consider suspending comments on psychotic material until later in the session. To what extent does your experience or training allow you to suspend assumptions until later? Role play a client with these difficulties with a colleague and consider the effect of solution questions on clients.

10

Generating hope with suicidal clients

Learning objectives

By the end of this chapter the reader will be able to assess the client using solution focused questions, in order to determine if the client is in the realms of management on safety grounds or therapy and formulate an appropriate course of action in each case. We will consider a separation between the clients' goal their means of achieving it. We aim to assist clients to focus on their goal and generate alternative pathways to it, rather than their initial route, suicide.

Rules of thumb with disclosures of suicidal intent

1. Wherever possible, suspend all assumptions about the meaning of the clients' words or the action to be taken until later in the session.
2. Continue with the Miracle, exception and scaling questions, which can generate ideas of what the client wants to be different about their lives.
3. This creates alternative pathways to achieve goals which may not best be met by suicide. For example, to want peace of mind, to be left alone by school bullies, to have a close relationship. Once these ends as we shall call them (peace, etc.) are established, the means (suicide) may not be as appropriate as less final alternatives. Is suicide the *only way of achieving their goal*?
4. Always consider client safety as paramount. If, by the end of the session, you are not confident that the clients can keep themselves free from harm, then your role changes from therapy to

management and the therapist needs to follow whatever professional or organizational policies are in place. This can include getting in touch with carers to inform them of the situation, contacting the GP or arranging for admission as a voluntary patient via psychiatric assessment and a section of the Mental Health Act or, occasionally, contacting the police where relevant. These actions should follow on from an exploration of the clients' goals (scaling questions focused on safety (discussed later) and the use of a risk assessment tool, whichever is favoured by your organization), not as a first reaction to suicidal disclosure.

5. Only use comments such as 'Think of your family', if the client has said that thinking of their family helps them overcome the urge to self harm. Leading the client with statements such as 'What about your daughter?', etc., carry moral and pejorative weight bear that may make the client feel worse about themselves. Our aim is to avoid increasing blame and guilt in clients who often feel to blame or guilty about even having such ideas.

Introduction

Psychiatry has had difficulty in developing a respectful reaction to people expressing ideas of suicide. This may be partly because of the anxiety these comments generate in the therapist. Traditionally, the immediate reaction has been to virtually stop the session, get a doctor in, consider a section of the Mental Health Act and have the client admitted to an inpatient ward. Even less overt reactions of 'panic' in a therapist when a client first mentions suicide as an option, can have the effect of closing the session down. Paradoxically, such reactions early in the session make it less likely that a client will be able to voice their feelings freely. As nurses, we have had clients respond to the question, 'Are you saying you might harm yourself at this time?' with the comment, 'If I tell you that, you will suggest admission and I don't want to go in'. Society has a problem with suicide, largely created by a kind of 'suicidal folklore' that is still, surprisingly, prevalent: 'People who talk about it won't do it'; 'Serious intent is marked by leaving a note'; 'All people who attempt suicide are of unsound mind'; 'You can't work therapeutically with suicidal clients'; 'Mentioning suicide, somehow, concretizes it and make it more likely that it will happen'.

Thinking about suicide is more prevalent than, perhaps, we would like to admit. This was brought home to the authors by a colleague, Len Collingwood, who says, 'It is a fortunate person who will get through their life without thinking about their own suicide at least once'. Prisoners of war have talked about the idea of suicide as the ultimate act of free will and control; the idea that they could take their own life was one that kept them alive in a situation where their captors controlled everything else about their existence. Many clients present with a similar idea that having suicide as a final option can make proceeding with life more tolerable, although, obviously, it would be nice for them to have motivations other than this for living.

It is a paradox that counselling and therapy attempts to encourage clients to talk honestly about their difficulties, but often cannot listen to the context or goals of their clients once suicide has been mentioned. Further reasons not to express suicidal ideas, we believe, are contained in the attempt to compartmentalize clients into 'suicide' and 'para-suicide'.

Most papers and published works attempt to differentiate between the terms 'suicide' and 'parasuicide'. Such definitions include parasuicide as '. . . any non fatal act of deliberate self-injury or taking of a substance (excluding alcohol) in excess of the general recognised or prescribed therapeutic dose'. (Kreitman and Dyer, 1980; quoted in 'Parasuicide' by Brooking and Minghella, 1987.) The authors go on to say that 'the parasuicide act does not, necessarily, involve an intention to commit suicide'.

'Parasuicide' as a term carried with it a stigma, an idea that the client 'didn't mean it' and, often, clients report feeling afterwards that they were treated badly by professionals who gave them the impression they were 'wasting their time'. As we have learned with words covered earlier in this book (such as, 'depression', 'manipulation' and 'psychosis') their meaning can, often, change during a solution focused conversation and if the Solution Therapist simply considers with the client what they want to achieve, and what their goals are by behaving in a particular manner, the original terms are no longer appropriate.

It has proved time consuming and problematic for all caring professions and models of therapy, to distinguish 'true suicidal intent' from a 'cry for help'. It is possible for people to commit suicide 'accidentally' were there is no true intent. For example, in *Savage God* by Alvarez (1974) Sylvia Plath is cited as having made suicidal attempts during her lifetime and being discovered 'by accident' when she had concealed herself well following overdoses. She died after, apparently, making every attempt to ensure she would be found, when her au pair was late returning home and never discovered her.

Similarly, there can be unintentional consequences of intentional parasuicidal behaviour, for example, unintended fatal consequences of paracetamol overdoses where the victim did not realize the dangerousness of such an everyday drug. There is also the concept of the 'rope of life', suggested by David Malan – the nearer a person gets to the fatal act, the more the life force will tend to pull them back from the brink, and the further away from suicide itself, the easier it is to plan the event and hold firm 'intent'. This, further, confuses the issue of intention in relation to final outcome. Someone can have a well founded intention to commit an act of suicide but when faced with the final action they may pull away from it. Does this mean they were not a serious risk?

Apparently, author Yukio Mishima was revered after his suicide in Japan because of the depth to which he had managed to push in the ceremonial sword during his act of Hara-kiri. This was in reference to his willpower in overcoming the 'rope of life' to such an extent.

Rather than attempting to create an academic division between the terms suicide and parasuicide, Solution Therapy takes everything the client says as serious and attempts to discover what the clients wants, and to find as many other ways to achieve this as possible. This introduces the notion of choice and with choice comes hope. Once you generate hope, you have a second session to help to preserve life.

Therapeutic activity

Statistics suggest at least 1,000,000 people in the UK deliberately harm themselves every year (Wells, 1981) and that far from being resistant or reluctant to receive any help, 'Most had visited their GPs recently . . . more than half had been or were, currently, receiving psychiatric care' (Brooking and Minghella, 1987).

There are two important components to work with this client group, management and therapy. These two actions are, often, unrelated. Solution focused questioning can be an aid to both, but actions may be different depending on which area of activity the client engages in.

Therapy

The standard solution focused interview is the therapist's starting point, regardless of diagnostic category. To some extent, every client is initially engaged in therapy. Solution questions are followed through logically and, only if the therapist still has concerns about safety at the end of the session or the client is still intent on following a course of action that the therapist cannot cooperate with (e.g., to take an overdose), therapy is no longer an option and management is necessary. Therapy is, therefore, assessment in itself, as well as treatment in this situation, and is our starting point.

Therapy involves working through the means of the client's solution (suicide as an answer to their present difficulties) to identify the ends behind this drive (to be happy, married, popular, respected, at peace, etc.).

'Suicidal patients have a specific deficit in problem solving skills' (Salkovskis *et al.*, 1989). It is this difficulty in generating alternative solutions to problems that the Miracle Question, exception questions and scaling questions help to redress.

By taking suicide as an attempted solution to a problem (but only one of many) you reduce blame for the client and value the difficult nature of their situation. You invite the client to wonder if this is the only valid solution. This can generate intrigue and curiosity which maximizes cooperation with the client, rather than causing them to have to explain the seriousness of the situation and the correctness of their choice. By investigating alternative solutions to the problem, and a different map for reaching their overall goal (other than self harm) you help the client feel valued and open up options.

Thus, an initial answer to the Miracle Question may be, 'if a miracle happened I'd be dead'. The therapist takes this answer as an indication of the seriousness of the situation but, again, does not panic. 'How would that help?' may produce the answer, 'My money worries would have gone', 'I'd have got some peace', 'I'd be less of a burden', 'My family would be off my back about my exam results', etc. Tracking and expanding these statements with 'How could you tell this was happening?', 'What would be the first sign that you were feeling more peaceful?', 'What else could you do to get some rest rather than harm yourself?', etc., begin to help the client see what they really want to be different, which is, actually, rarely 'to be dead'.

They begin to separate suicide (the act) from what they want to be different (which may have nothing to do with death). Exception questions and scaling questions introduce the idea of movement and possibility. It is important to focus these questions, specifically, around the issue of suicide; 'Are there any times when you have felt, recently, that it is really worth carrying on living?'. As with other answers to the 'miracle', the broader the picture that is generated in terms of relationship questions, 'What else would be different?', 'Who else would notice that you have begun to sort out this problem?', 'who else?', etc., the greater the potential for generating hope and alternative options.

The scales and 'What would be the first step towards this, apart from self harm, be?' questions, help the client to see other routes to these goals without having to choose the final path of suicide. The fact that independence, strength, peace of mind and less arguments with your family are possible, and possible in other ways, helps to slowly generate hope without blame. The acceptance of suicidal thoughts as an alternative, but only one of many alternatives, supports the client in how difficult things have been. When scaling, clients will, usually, be low on these scales and may be in 'minus' situations, but may surprise the therapist by stating things like:

CL: 'I'm on minus 4.'
TH: 'Is this the lowest you have been?'
CL: 'No, last week I'd say I was at minus 8.'
TH: What's changed that has allowed you to hang on and move up to minus 4?'

Expect low scores and pace slower than usual to ensure that the clients feel heard and respected; that your pace matches them rather than trying to 'look on the bright side'.

Scaling questions on risk assessment

As well as the usual solution focused questions ('willingness to do', 'confidence' and 'Where are you now?') particular questions about risk are applicable:

'On a scale of 0 to 10 what are the chances (or how likely is it) that you will kill yourself?'
'What are the changes that I could dissuade you from this?'
'Who is the most likely person around for you, to help you hold on and give you a reason to live?'
'What are the chances that someone else, or something else, can dissuade you from this?'
'On a scale of 0 to 10 how worried should I be about you?'
'If you are on 0 at the moment, what would a half look like, something that would help you move, minimally, forward?'
'What difference would this make?'
'On a scale of 0 to 10, how much do you want to find an alternative to this situation?'
(A low scale answer to this question would indicate management may be necessary.)
'On a scale where 0 was where you felt very unsafe and 10 was that you were as safe as you could be, what would 10 look like?', 'Who would be around?', 'Where would you be?', 'What would be happening?', etc. (A description of a safest alternative may help determine the course of action for the family to take to secure the client, or the therapist to take in order to ensure safety.)
'How realistic is it that you can stay safe this weekend?'
'How confident are you that you can stay safe this weekend?'

Empowering questions

A lot of therapy attempts to persuade clients not to feel as bad as they do. Solution Therapy gives clients permission to feel as bad as they do. It is not our role to dissuade them from the intensity of their feelings, only to help them find a different way of coping with these feelings. By giving permission to feel bad over traumatic life events, you humanize these feelings, introduce the idea that they may be universal and that anyone could feel as bad, given the same circumstances. Dealing with the issues in this way can help a client feel less isolated. As well as the risk assessment questions above, empowering questions can follow them, such as:

> 'This must be an unbelievable experience for you, a nightmare. Knowing yourself as you do, what have you learned about yourself that has allowed you to get this far with the problem?'
> 'How come you got here to see me today?', 'How come you have held on?', 'How have you resisted it so far?'
> 'Does it surprise you that you have been this strong, that even given this you are still around?', 'What about others in your life, would they have known that you were as strong as this?'

It is often worth the therapist remembering Ben Furman's words in *Solution Talk*, 'Traumatic experiences can be a source of learning as well as a source of distress' (Furman and Ahola, 1992, p. 37). Therefore, we would be curious about what the client has learned about themselves that had enabled them to resist giving in to these urges so far.

Consistently low answers to these scales may indicate that the client is set on a path of self harm as a solution. The therapist, then, has to move on to management since they can no longer cooperate with this goal and the client is, in effect, in a visitor relationship.

Time frames can also be considered, e.g., 'Is this something that will take more time to solve?', 'Are you being hard on yourself, expecting yourself to feel very different that this?'. This gives permission to feel as bad as they do.

Management

If death is really the only goal, then the therapist needs to manage the client until they are able to ensure their own safety. The therapist can acknowledge that they have to do this to the client and be open about the fact they cannot sit by and watch the client harm themselves. Management includes doing whatever at risk assessment is necessary, contacting other professionals and acting to preserve life. The client simply has a goal you cannot cooperate with and therapy is not as paramount an issue as immediate safety.

Exercise

What do you think when you hear the word 'suicide'? One thing is for certain, it conjures up strong emotions. Consider a solution session with a suicidal client. How could the use of exceptions and logic help clients? How do you, personally, decide risk? Role play a session with a 'suicidal' colleague, keeping to the model, and assess its impact on the client and therapist.

11

Inpatient and statutory settings

Learning objectives

The use of the approach on wards in residential units is considered. Readers will be aware of adaptations to the formal session that can allow Solution Therapy in this setting.

Flexible Model Formal Setting

Solution Focused Therapy is flexible enough to be used as a therapeutic tool in statutory settings and on hospital wards. Successful application of solution focused ideas have been reported by staff in Montrose, Hereford and Worcester, USA and Brugge.

The main benefits of the approach are that it is able to be used in conjunction with other therapies including medication. Its logical stance allows a respectful management role to be a possibility until therapy is again appropriate and the questions stand on their own, allowing short therapeutic conversations outside of a formal 'hour-long session'.

Solution focused questions can be asked outside of the structure of a formal session. Insoo Kim Berg wrote guidelines for the 20-minute interview and Ron Kral (1982, discussion with authors) stated that he used the questions within a school setting, simply asking scales and Miracle Questions in the corridor (prompting cries of 'I'm at a 9, Ron' or 'I'm at a 7, Ron' whenever he passed by!).

Admission routines and assessment interviews provide ideal situations to use solution focused questions. One of the first questions that can be asked of a newly admitted client to an acute psychiatric unit is: 'What needs to be different in your life in order that you can leave here?', or 'What would your wife see that would tell her that you are really ready to go home and she needn't worry about you as much?'. Given that they are currently removed from their community, not only would the client and therapist construct what needs to be different about the client's life outside of the institution and how that could be achieved in the long-term future, but also what immediate changes can they make that would indicate to themselves and to the ward staff that they are ready for discharge?

The client's response to the Miracle Question can be documented verbatim and used as a negotiated goal for treatment.

The answers to exception and scaling questions represent steps towards health and independent functioning and as such can be entered as part of the client's individual care plan, with actions by staff to help this be identified and dated. This makes review of progress easier since the practitioner has the client's scales from admission as well as the institution's 'contract of care' and can easily assess how much movement has occurred. If the institution uses admissions documentation there are spaces for the client's responses to the Miracle, exception and scaling questions to be recorded.

The answer to the Miracle, scaling and relationship questions provide the practitioner with small behavioural steps towards mental health that are described in measurable terms and are negotiated with the client. This forms the seeds of any good care plan and so the activities of interviewing/assessing and documenting can be rolled into one.

If answers to the solution focused questions are delusional or psychotic they can still be entered as clinical information since such material would be entered notes anyway as an indication of mental state on admission. At worst, the model provides useful assessment questions and, at best, the process of negotiating goals and orienting the client towards change and discharge is begun at the admission interview through using these questions.

Careful consideration of the visitor/customer/complainant relationship is needed here since clients may be required to stay in these settings regardless of their own wishes. In these cases the agency's guidelines and therapist's responsibilities to their work settings are uppermost but as we have seen it may still be possible to interest the client in an 'alternative goal', aimed at making their stay as short as possible and improving their quality of life. Work with families and diagnosis such as 'psychosis' is covered elsewhere and sometimes the customer relationship is with the relatives of the client, since they are more able to accept psychological support than the client.

As we have said, goals such as 'I'd get out of here' are seen as appropriate starting places for work rather than evidence of resistance: as are questions such as, 'What has to happen before the staff here feel confident that you could cope on the outside?' and 'What do you think we would have to see that's different about you that would tell us there is the beginning of change?'.

Ward staff we trained in Montrose related the story of using the Miracle Question with a man admitted to the ward under a Section of the Mental Health Act. For him, the 'miracle' would be 'My arse would stop melting'. The ward staff asked, 'What else?' and followed up on relationship/exception questions. Other realistic goals then appeared. It is this ability to track carefully whatever clients say and continue with the model even when the answers to questions are not what the therapist hopes for that is necessary in statutory settings. Staff developing a unified approach to therapy, with support of each team member and joint understanding of Solution Focused Therapy (preferably with staff team training events on the approach and its aims) are essential components if the model is to be used successfully in statutory settings. It does not have to be applied 'religiously' since brief conversations may be sufficient. Also, as the questions are 'non-toxic' in nature they provide a useful starting point for junior staff.

Statutory duties are often: (a) to manage clients; and (b) to do so in a respectful manner that introduces alternatives to present behaviours, thoughts and feelings. Solution Focused ideas about future orientation and collaboration until a joint goal can be found can add creativity and hope to clients while accepting the responsibility of care. The concept of visitor relationships helps staff not to expect too much from their clients and to accept that they may have other goals to the institution's goals.

For clients who are on medication the question is, 'Is it working?', and if so, 'What is it helping the clients to do?'. In our experience, clients become curious about their ability to manage without medication and we encourage them to seek medical guidance on this. For clients who are certain that medicine does not help them, when there is family evidence, GP letters and clinical material that suggests medication *is* helpful, you are in the realm of management and must carry out management duties according to your organization's requirements, but helpful starting questions are: 'If you had to stay on medication a bit longer, what else could you do to help yourself?' or, 'What would convince your family, GP or us that you no longer need the medication?'.

Staff often report difficulty in maintaining session boundaries if they are engaged in everyday activities with clients as well as a 40-minute or so 'formal' session each week. It does help to ask 'What's better?', or

'How's things?' when meeting the client outside of sessions and respond to any answers by saying, 'We'll talk about this at more length when we next meet'. Although formal boundaries are not as important with this model it does help to create some space in between contacts during which the client can think about the questions themselves and work on issues without having the therapist to turn to too frequently.

There may be circumstances when the institution/organization's goals may be radically different from the client's goals and there may be no possibility of fit or compromise. In these circumstances, the staff members' responsibilities to protect clients' safety, to keep to their professional code of conduct, to their employers, to the public, etc., override the responsibility to perform therapy.

Therapists should be sure they know what their role is in statutory work (e.g., to protect children or prevent self harm) and while they may still be able to use solution focused questions they may not be able to cooperate with a client's goal. Again, the 'non-miracle' scenario (explained in Chapter 6) comes into play.

In summary, Solution Therapy, with its flexibility to other treatments and its ability to try and find alternative goals that may interest those in a visitor relationship, is suitable to statutory settings. It is easily translated into usable documentation that marries assessment, treatment and administration and, while being logical enough to accept that management may be more necessary than therapy, still attempts to develop goals that the client and the therapist can cooperate on in order to help clients move towards more control, independence and health in their lives.

Exercises

Consider the Miracle Question and scales as separate entities that can be used in separate conversations with clients. Consider the basic assumptions of the approach again and their suitedness to a residential philosophy of care. Consider residential admission/assessment procedures. Is there room in the assessment interview for the Miracle Question and scales (to develop fast-care plans with clients)?

12

Comments on
Solution Focused Group Therapy

Learning objectives

Readers will be aware of the approach's suitability for group work and differences in technique that such work demands.

When we initially discussed group therapy with Steve de Shazer in 1992 he was unsure if an adaptation to groups was possible. His concern was rooted in the fact that the model was entered in individual conversations and negotiation through language. It was unclear how this could be translated to a group of unrelated individuals.

Since 1993 we have been applying Solution Focused Therapy in a group situation in an acute psychiatric day hospital. This largely came about as a result of clients requesting therapy that would help them to move away from their problem and forward towards the rest of their life. Several were expressing a frustration at being in group therapies for 12 to 18 months, exploring their past and their relationships and understanding possible causes for their problem, but feeling no better or clearer about what to do as a result of it.

Thoughts about adaptation to groups

Because we know that Solution Focused Therapy focuses on the construction, through language, of mutually defined problems and goals it would be difficult to replicate this in a large group setting without undertaking individual therapy with 15 different people, 14 of whom would be observers at any one time. Therefore, we looked at how we could transfer the spirit of the model into the group situation. We reasoned that central solution focused questions could be productive and so we kept:

'What's brought you here?'
'How do you want to be helped by attending the group?'
'What have you tried so far that is already working for you?'
Miracle Question.
Exception questions.
Where are you now scale.
Motivation scale.
Confidence scale.
Feedback on next steps.

The important relationship with this application of the model has been 'the group as therapist'. In keeping with the client as expert and the open equal nature of the solution focused therapeutic relationship we invited clients to split into sub-groups and interview each other, with the therapists acting as convenor, time-keeper and supervisor. In effect each group is a 'mini-workshop' where clients become familiar with solution focused ideas while taking it in turns to help each other.

The group convenes for feedback after a specified amount of time to share their individual objectives, the 'next step', and how much time they think they require to do this. Should the sub-groups require any specific information to help an individual (e.g., relaxation tapes, book lists, etc.) the therapist is prepared to act as librarian, advocate and facilitator. The therapist may occasionally be requested to conduct a small group interview if the group becomes stuck, but the group is asked to contribute as an observing team with suggestions and questions.

What we learned

We encountered various pitfalls when setting up the group. Initially we structured a 'closed group' in which clients were allowed to attend for 15 sessions and were expected to attend every session. Both expectations run counter to the philosophy of this approach because the therapist was taking responsibility for the number of sessions and the frequency of attendance. Once we realized that we had taken this stance, we corrected it and made the group an 'open group' in which clients could commence membership at any point, although the maximum number of members would not exceed 15, which we saw to be an optimum size to facilitate 'supervision' of the small group work.

It was also necessary for the clients to have a choice in discerning how frequently they needed to attend. This means that any one group session will have a membership ranging from 3 or 4 to the maximum 15 as clients either terminate or take 'time out' from the therapy.

Group members can be therapists to other members. Although the flexible nature of the group develops its own culture, this culture does not fit neatly into Yallom's (1931) categorization of the curative factors in groups which were:

catharsis;
universality;
developments of appropriate social interaction techniques;
group cohesion;
altruism;
the corrective re-enactment of the primary family group;
existential factors;
imitative behaviours;
interpersonal learning;
instillation of hope.

Yallom felt these factors were essential for a therapeutic group experience. Although some of these factors are present in a solution focused group they do not appear to be necessary pre-requisites for a therapeutic outcome.

Groups lasted an hour with an introduction, feedback from the week and a discussion with the group actually helping to interview each member and pick up on the positives, exceptions, scales and steps left to go. The group then allowed individuals to set tasks for themselves and discussed the realism of these.

Summary

Solution Focused Therapy works well in groups although the ground rules developed may be different both from traditional forms of group therapy and also from traditional ideas about how Solution Therapy is practised. Groups take on a 'workshop' feel with clients being taught the techniques and then taking on much of the interviewing with each other. Art could become a part of the process, allowing groups another medium to explore miracles with group collages of a miracle talked through during the latter part of the session. Whole sessions devoted to exploring the Miracle Question were not uncommon and wall charts, paper and pens for writing down group ideas and displaying them can prove useful.

Exercises

Consider the application to a group of your clients. Would you use stricter boundaries of other media (art, drama, writing, etc.) to develop the richness of the Miracle Question?

What about clients being taught the model in order to have input with each other in sub-groups? Would clients interviewing each other under supervision be helpful? Is that a concept that would fit within your work setting?

13

Philosophy of the approach

Learning objectives

This chapter concerns itself with a brief overview of the philosophies behind Solution Focused Therapy. It aims to explain why we believe what clients say, and interview to get a detailed description of what they want rather than searching for their 'real problems' or seeing their requests (e.g., 'I would like to have more friends and go out more') as evidence of underlying shyness, anxiety, earlier experiences or pathology. It covers structuralism, and post-structuralism briefly to allow a comparison of traditional psychodynamic or behavioural approaches and Solution Focused Therapy, and quotes from Wittgenstein and Derrida, the philosophers de Shazer links most closely to Solution Focused Therapy. By the end of the chapter the reader should be able to consider post-structural thinking and give a rationale for Solution Therapy's focus on descriptions (surface structure) rather than causes or meanings (deep structure).

Not a great deal has been written about the underlying philosophy of Solution Focused Therapy until recently. Therapy can be described as falling into two schools of thought, structural thinking and post-structural thinking.

Structural thought

Structural thinking is embodied in our ideas about science. Scientific thought sees the world as something that can be measured, gathered into theories, and that predictions can be made about events if they are carefully observed and recorded. Freud followed the 'scientific revolution' himself. Trained as a biologist, his theories gave a structure of the mind (Id, Ego, Super Ego, or conscious subconscious, and unconscious) whose symptoms are observable manifestations of internal conflicts and anxieties. What the client says becomes 'evidence' for the skilled therapist to uncover causes of behaviour and/or meanings behind these events. In short there is a reality and this reality can be understood and discovered but the therapist must 'read between the lines'.

You have the 'surface structure' when the client says, 'I am depressed' and the therapist must go beneath what the client says in order to understand what the client means: 'How long have you felt this way, tell me about your life, etc.' The therapist will then try and discover what caused the depression.

'The Structuralists, in general, are concerned to *know* the (human) world – to uncover it through detailed observational analysis and to map it out under extended explanatory grids. Their stance is still the traditional scientific goal of truth' (Harland, 1987). The 'truth' is in the sub-structure of events and not on the surface. What is happening for a client can only be gleaned by looking behind and beneath words and behaviour. The therapist, thanks to experience and skill, can uncover the cause and meaning for the client. Therefore, it is the 'meaning' between, behind and beneath the words of a client that tell us about their problem.

Structuralism is evident in Western thinking, and is found in any therapy that is interested in a 'cause' or prescribes a set treatment to solve a problem, such as the Medical Model, Psychoanalysis, Family Therapy, Behavioural Psychotherapy, Rogerian therapy. Structural thinking, while being essential in the everyday physical world (identifying a problem with your car, taking the engine apart and fixing a broken hidden component causing a rattle) can be seen to be rather more uncertain when dealing with the psychological world, with ideas such as 'confidence', 'depression' or 'alcoholism'.

Harland (1987) suggests that post-structuralism is: 'Not only incompatible with the concept of structure but also radically anti-scientific'. Perhaps this explains how post-structuralism is so difficult to grasp (or explain) since we have all been trained in more structural ideas and they are familiar to us. This example of a hypothetical solution focused interview leads us on to a further examination of post-structural thought. Solution Therapy leads us on to the second.

Post-structural thought

Post-structural thought believes that there may be many different realities. The meaning of words and events can be 'constructed', discussed and agreed on by a process of negotiation. Therefore how accurate a diagnosis of 'depression' is can be discussed and agreed. Meaning can be decided upon by those present according to fit and usefulness rather than interpretation or 'facts'. To paraphrase Watzlawick, 'Reality is invented rather than discovered' (Watzlawick, 1984). There are, therefore, many 'truths' and many reasons for behaviour, and cause and effect are more difficult to determine.

> For the structuralist, meanings are stable and knowable . . . for the Post structuralist, meaning is seen as known through social interaction and negotiation; Meaning here is open to view since it lies between people rather than hidden away inside an individual.
>
> (de Shazer, 1991, p. 45)

> While structuralism sees truth as being 'behind' or 'within' a text, post structuralism stresses the interaction of reader and text as productivity.
>
> (Sarup, 1989, p. 3)

Therapists cannot know what is going to be helpful in a given case from experience or skill. It is the client, not the therapist, who is the expert in their difficulty. Further, more looking 'beneath' what people say for clues to the 'real cause' of a difficulty is seen as essentially guess-work. Listening to the description of what the client wants is the important thing rather than interpreting or 'guessing' at what the client 'really' is telling us. Therefore, we are interested in the description of what they want rather than assuming what a 'real' problem or 'underlying cause' might be. If the client says they want to sleep better we look at this; if they say their anxiety at work needs to change, we work on this.

De Shazer (1991) gives an example of how post-structuralist thinking would deal with the same client's statement, 'I am depressed'.

> Suppose that you came to me as a client. You can know that you are depressed. So far your experience has fit with that idea, that knowledge. Nothing has happened to you that suggests that you are wrong. Your view of yourself fits within the constraints of your environment, allowing you to predict certain things: your response to efforts to cheer you up and other people's response to your being down.

You say to me 'I am depressed'. I know that you know that, but I do not know from your statement that you are depressed. The words 'depressed' and 'depression' are not depression itself. So, given my 20 years of experience, I wonder how you are using that word. I ask, 'How do you know you are depressed?'. At that point you need to use some criteria, some evidence that will support your knowledge and use of the word 'depressed'.

You might say in support of your knowledge that you know you are depressed right now, 'because I've been depressed all my life'. However, this undermines and contaminates your statement, 'I am depressed', because you might use the word 'depressed' as equivalent to the word 'normal'. For me, the statement that you have been depressed all of your life is no criterion for using the word 'depressed'; it is not evidence for being depressed right now because you might have been mistaken all your life. Therefore, I ask, 'How do you know that?'.

Now you are probably wondering about how you will ever know you are depressed; therefore, you say, 'I never get anything done. I either sleep too much or have difficulty sleeping and I either gorge myself or starve myself'. OK, now both you and I are starting to have some ideas about how you are using the word 'depressed'. We may agree or disagree about your use of that word, we may agree to use some other word(s), or you may continue to use that word while I call it something else.

I might ask, 'When was the most recent time when you were not aware that you were depressed?'. You search your memory and say, 'Oh, last Tuesday'. This further contaminates and undermines your use of the words 'always depressed' and so sparks my curiosity. I ask, 'What did you do last Tuesday?'. You say, 'I got up early and played golf for the first time in eight months' and I will say, 'What else was different on last Tuesday?'. 'I went out for pizza and beers, danced with a couple of girls and fell asleep on the couch before I went to bed.'

Within the context of this imaginary conversation, we both know that your use of the word depressed is different from your criteria for saying that you are not depressed and now we have criteria for both concepts. Together we have constructed a meaning for your use of the word depressed that includes (1) *not* playing golf, (2) *not* going out for pizza and beer, (3) *not* dancing with girls, and (4) *not* spontaneously falling asleep on the couch before you are ready for bed. This definition, that we have agreed you mean by your use of the word depressed, may or may not have been part of the meaning that you brought with you into the session and it may or may not have been part of the meaning I brought into the session.

(de Shazer, 1991, pp. 47–8)

Wittgenstein identified the idea that there is no need to go 'underneath' language. 'We are not concerned with anything hidden, because everything lies "open to view". Instead of penetrating vision, what we want is to command a clear view. It is true in a sense there is something "hidden" but not because it lies beneath the surface: rather, it is because it is right on the surface, in plain sight' (Staten, 1984). By focusing on what the client wants initially it may evolve that the client also wants their marriage to change or to come to terms with a loss (that there is some other difficulty to be worked with), etc., but it also may not.

De Shazer would suggest that if there is not enough information, instead of giving in to the temptation to go behind and beneath what clients say to search for meaning and cause, we continue to ask the client questions to get a clearer picture through conversation about what they want to happen. Instead of asking why, we say, 'After the miracle how will things be different?', listen to their answer and try and help them achieve what they say they want.

Solution focused thinking

Traditional therapy approaches are informed by theories of 'personality development' or 'problem development'. Symptoms of psychological distress in these frameworks are causally linked to ways of thinking, biochemical difficulties or previous life events. The solution focused approach does not necessarily hold to any of these ideas. In a sense, Solution Therapy can be seen to be agnostic as to whether psychology fails (where it fails) because the links it makes are correct or incorrect; too involved or too parsimonious. Evidence from practice indicates that on numerous occasions these links; true or false are merely unnecessary.

The Solution Focused Practitioner is essentially disinterested in any idea relating to causality (at least for the duration of the interviews); he devotes himself to 'co-constructing' possible solutions which may have no connection to the presenting problem.

Since we believe reality is a construction in which the client plays an equal part, we enter into conversations focused on using language to construct a preferred scenario. Our conversations are about change, confidence, times when the client brought their own strengths to bear on the problem and how they would know they were better. The more we talk about these issues the more real these possibilities become for the client.

We also suspend as many of our assumptions about the client, their diagnosis, the possible outcome of therapy, the 'usefulness' or 'appropriateness' of Solution Focused Therapy with 'this kind of client', etc., until later. Jacques Derrida suggests that it is the reader, not the writer, of a text that attributes the meaning to words. The writer only discovers the meaning of his words in the act of writing them. The reader brings their own feelings, interpretation, beliefs and experiences to the written word and may perceive a different meaning than that intended by the author. This is similar in spoken language and, as such, we can only discover the meaning of a diagnostic label such as 'obsessive compulsive disorder' through conversing with the client about what they want, rather than accepting the label as the truth.

We are often tempted to act on a diagnostic label or case history as if we knew how it applied to that person, as if everyone was the same and may even decide this will be a 'difficult case' or this model is 'unsuitable' before meeting the client.

In short, we advocate an individualist stance, where the meanings we bring to the therapy about diagnostic labels and appropriate treatments, etc., are suspended since we will discover what the meaning of 'alcoholism' or 'depression' may be through interviewing the client. The meaning of these words will be different every time, with every new client, as will the solution – since every new client brings unique abilities, knowledge and ideas to bear on a problem.

In fact, we may discover what 'depression' means to the client by getting a description of its opposite, by using the Miracle, relationship and scaling questions to develop a picture of how life could be. Logically, if not being depressed is playing golf, going out for a pizza and dancing with girls then being depressed may be not doing these things! De Shazer quotes Wittgenstein as saying, 'The only interesting thing about a problem is that it carries within itself an idea of a solution. If I know about being depressed I must also know about what not being depressed would look like.' Solution Focused Therapy looks at the not being depressed side of the coin. If necessary (for paperwork, etc.) you can derive the 'depressed' side from asking about this side.

While other therapies are influenced by various causal theories, Solution Focused Therapy is influenced by aspects of linguistic philosophy, which emphasize the representational function of language above all else, and would be chary of assuming it corresponds with any underlying reality.

Wittgenstein's rhinoceros and how language can become 'real'

The approach draws on the work of Wittgenstein who maintained in a famous interchange with Bertrand Russell that language itself does not represent reality but constructs reality (this discussion was recreated in the 1993 film 'Wittgenstein', Connoisseur Video). We need look no further than the labels 'schizophrenic' and 'alcoholic' to discover what Wittgenstein may have meant. Each of these terms may carry connotations, memories, reservations, predicted behaviours, treatment options, limitations of treatment, etc., with them. The labels in a sense become as 'real' as the client they represent because the experience and assumptions of the therapist are called into being with the terms used. A kind of reality is created, where the therapist (if they are not careful to 'suspend' their assumptions until after meeting the client and talking with them) can believe that these terms describe the client accurately and that they represent real problems the client has (rather than being simply words).

Wittgenstein illustrated the 'reality' of words by arguing that there was 'a rhinoceros in the room' with himself and Russell. Russell found no empirical evidence to prove it but, nevertheless, the idea of the presence of the animal was the topic of conversation and in a sense each man had the image of it in his head where none existed before the word 'magicked' the unlikely topic of conversation out of thin air.

Summary

Solution Focused Therapy is considered a post-structural approach. It does not try and ask questions about cause and effect but instead tries to explore different aspects of what is happening for the client when he or she is not having the problem. It is in essence a surface activity and is not involved in issues of making hypotheses about reasons for these behaviours. Clinically the therapist:

1. as far as is possible suspends assumptions of hypothesis about the client;
2. deals with what the client says the difficulty is;
3. deals with surface descriptions of future behaviours in detail, rather than looking for depth explanations about causes;
4. assumes a 'not knowing' stance, rather than assuming they can help or can't help based on prior experience or theories.

Exercise

Consider the implications of post-structuralist thought to the concepts of 'diagnosis' and certainty in the caring professions. How could we read 'schizophrenia' with any confidence if influenced by these ideas? Suggested reading includes de Shazer, *Putting Difference to Work* (1991) and Watzlawick (ed) (1990), *Munchausen's Pigtail or Psychotherapy and Reality*.

14

Clinical case examples

Learning objectives

Full case examples are now presented so that the reader can consider, amongst other things, pacing and staying on track when the client presents multiple difficulties or the use of the model in 'difficult cases'. Clients should not be hurried and in some cases the clarification of what is to happen in therapy may take a couple of sessions. The therapist tries to match the pace of the questions and the size of scales to the client's predicament and the seriousness of the problem. Cases are presented on self harm, multiple difficulties and psychosis as examples of the models used in these areas. Readers should form an overall picture of the approach, pace and style of the therapist. The longer format should allow readers to 'track' the session with the therapist and consider the timing of the questions and the way that logical issues are raised. They should draw on the previous chapters to place these sessions in the context of the theory.

Practice

Practitioners can read a wealth of material on a model but it is only through role play at workshops or tentatively using new techniques that they can discover the benefits or drawback of a particular approach and assess how it fits with their style of interviewing. Case examples so far have been short and interspersed with comments to highlight technique. To help the reader get an idea of pacing and the 'clusters' of question we include some longer case studies with later discussion.

The idea of matching the client's pacing (if they are negative or the difficulties seem insurmountable the therapist slows down, listens more and asks for small differences in the scales, etc.) and that 'What you get is what you get', to paraphrase de Shazer, are highlighted. If life is difficult and there are multiple problems, then that is simply how things are for that client at that time and the therapist will work on 'What helps you cope?' questions to help the client get through each day, and later to make small changes.

Case example 1

Theresa

Theresa is a young, single woman referred to our clinic by a consultant psychiatrist following attempts at self harm, overdoses and unpredictable behaviour. She had been living abroad and working as a member of staff in a university when the problems necessitated admission to a private hospital abroad. She was admitted as an inpatient and given a variety of treatments including Electro Convulsive Therapy (ECT). Finally she was advised to return home on leave from her job to get treatment in Britain as her insurance cover had run out. On her return she was assessed thoroughly by both GP and psychiatrist who advised Solution Focused Therapy and was willing to admit her to the ward if this did not help her gain some control on her life. She had agreed with the psychiatrist not to attempt self harm again while in therapy and a full risk assessment was carried out prior to the solution sessions, thus keeping the 'problem focused' risk assessment and psychiatric functions separate from the 'solution building' activities of these sessions. She had a return ticket for eight weeks' time and intended to return to her academic life abroad then.

Session 1

CL: (On entering the room) 'Can I just ask if you are a doctor or what you are?'

TH: 'I'm a psychiatric nurse' (shares his qualifications and explains the structure of the session, screen, team, etc.).

CL: 'Thanks, it's just that I have seen so many people recently and they are passing me to someone new every time. I feel I've been assessed but I'm not getting anything after that.'

TH: 'OK. What has brought you here today?'

CL: 'I have been seeing the doctor because of depression.'
TH: 'How would you like us to help – what would be helpful?'
CL: 'I want help but I do not know if you can help me with the problems.'
TH: 'You want them sorted?'
CL: 'I had a breakdown in August, I was in hospital for one month. I've just come back from abroad one-and-a-half weeks ago. I was hospitalized due to depression but my insurance ran out. They were even giving me ECT: I got to 8; they wanted to give me 14. I'd been in one month and my insurance was only for 30 days, so the choice was come back to England or go into a state hospital. They did not want this and so the doctor suggested I come back to England. I would rather be back over there. I took a leave of absence for three or more months (unpaid). The doctor over there said I should come back and be hospitalized, I was really bad. I saw my GP and he got in touch with the psychiatrist. I cannot remember this as the treatment screwed my head up.'
TH: 'Did ECT help?'
CL: 'No'
TH: 'Have you tried anything else?'
CL: 'Anti-depressants and tranquillizers. The doctor has taken me off them and now I'm on one tranquillizer, Melleril. Apparently, I tried to take a knife to myself but I do not remember. My brother had to hold me down, I was taken to hospital here and seen. When I was abroad I tried to kill myself. I cannot remember much but at present I feel like I want to die.'
TH: 'Imagine you go from here today and you go to sleep and when you sleep a miracle happens and life is how you want it to be. When you woke up tomorrow morning what would be the first thing you would notice that would tell you something is a little different today?'
CL: 'That I will have the will to live. I am not looking for anything else, only the will to live. I would wake up and want to live.'
TH: 'What difference will this make to you?'
CL: 'I think it would be my work, I would be able to carry on with it. I'm a researcher and I'd like to get into some kind of medicine.'
TH: 'You can then pursue the career?'
CL: 'I guess I'm happy with my career at the moment, but then again I guess I'm not . . . it's all a bit confused.'
TH: 'You are on a leave of absence at the moment from work so what would be any immediate difference you would notice?'
CL: 'I just cry all the time and my tolerance level is so low I'm so negative. I have a different personality to six months ago. I shout, scream, argue and fly off the handle. This is not me at all, I'm

agitated all the time. One minute want to kill someone the next minute I'm elated. I do not understand it, it's difficult to understand.'

TH: 'You want to wake up and want to live and be stable?'

CL: 'Even though I have had problems all my life this is just magnified. I cannot cope. I don't care about anything.'

TH: 'What other things would need to be different if you were back on track?'

CL: 'I would just want to live. I don't know if I want to live. Just to find someone who can help me want to live.'

TH: 'Do you suppose you will wake up one day and you will want to live? Do you need to feel this is to change your life, or do you need to do things differently in some way so life is more worth living?'

CL: 'Maybe, I don't know. You see, I have had anorexia, bulimia, I use alcohol and I'm obsessional.'

TH: 'Do you have these problems at the moment?'

CL: 'The anorexia was worse, no . . . actually I think the bulimia was worse. I want to drink all the time and I am not meant to drink but it makes me want to drink more. I don't care.'

TH: 'That sounds pretty frustrating.'

CL: 'Yes it is but I still drink it.'

TH: 'What would your father notice was different?'

CL: 'I don't have much contact with my family. I moved when I was seventeen. I saw them once a year.'

TH: 'You are staying with them?'

CL: 'Staying with my mother. I would prefer not to, it does not help the situation, I would rather not be here. I am happy abroad. Here are too many bad memories where my parents are concerned and it's aggravating the situation especially with my father. Over the past couple of days I really hate him. I would pick up a knife and stab him sometimes. Maybe this is crazy. I am afraid I will do something, maybe take a knife to myself or take an overdose.'

TH: 'Harming yourself seems safer than harming anyone else?'

CL: 'It's worrying me. I have been here one-and-a-half weeks. I think I could stand in the doctor's office with a knife to my throat and they'd just say, "Go on keep taking the tablets", or something. On Monday, I don't know but maybe I would have done it. My brother was terrified, my mother was in a terrible state when I came round. I don't remember this like I do not recall the time before I was admitted, being overdosed with alcohol and the police taking me with handcuffs.'

TH: 'Have there been times, Theresa, when you have wanted to kill yourself and you have resisted the urge to harm yourself?'

CL: 'Well, yes, now. I have not thought about it in that way. I really don't want to do it when anybody is there. I wanted to stay abroad. I would take a bottle of vodka and overdose there but everybody was round me the whole time as soon as I got out of hospital. I could not go to my apartment, they would not let me be on my own, my mother flew over and that was worse. She would not return unless I came back with her. Also, I did not want to lose my job. I tried to commit suicide with alcohol again.'

TH: 'What would you need to come into your life to make carrying on a bit more worthwhile, even as a first step?'

CL: 'I guess I am waiting for someone to help me, to tell me that.'

TH: 'OK, so that's a bit of a grey area, you're not sure what will happen. Do you feel better some days compared with others?'

CL: 'My memory is not so good, I barely remember yesterday. Every morning I wake up the first thing I think is, "How do I feel today?", and it's just the same. I don't want to bother with anything, I want to put my head under the pillow to suffocate myself.'

TH: 'Every morning?'

CL: 'Every day. It just goes up and down. I'm not interested in anything, I cannot look at the television or the newspaper.'

TH: 'You were saying a number of things that worry you. Do you suppose that if these were to be sorted you would feel better?'

CL: 'I do not know if they can be sorted out.'

TH: 'You said about your eating pattern, that was worse. Suppose there were changes here and that was not so sensitive?'

CL: 'It seems to me if it's not one thing it's something else. I had anorexia, then bulimia, then I was beginning to get depressed and then went through a phase of – I don't know – afraid to go out and when I did go out I was terrified. It was lucky my supervisor was in England and I got away with not always going into work. It seems to me that if you cure one thing something else comes along.'

TH: 'That is what has happened up to now?'

CL: 'Anorexia and depression, they got better, then bulimia, then that – what's it called? – a fear of going into spaces, then depression, not sleeping and eating.'

TH: 'When was the last time you felt OK about yourself?'

CL: 'I think you learn to cope with these things. I think it was last year. But then I was in an earthquake, I really thought I was going to die and I went downhill.'

TH: 'When this seemed better, last year, what was different?'
CL: 'I was not so depressed. I did not want to commit suicide for over four months. I was more satisfied with things I suppose.'
TH: 'What made you feel more satisfied?'
CL: 'Nothing I can think of. My head seems to be screwed up, which it was not before.'
TH: 'On a scale of 0 to 10, when 10 was where you want to be and 0 was the problem at its worst, where would you say you are?'
CL: '0, if I was not dead.'
TH: 'So it's hard enough just getting through each day. What would tell you that it had moved up just a little bit?'
CL: 'Again, if I did not have this thing about wanting to die, that it does not matter. If I felt I just wanted to be here next year.'
TH: 'Maybe that feeling is a bit higher up at 3 or 4? What will tell you if it moved a little bit, just a quarter of a point up that scale?'
CL: 'Cannot think now. Before I was able to get up in the morning, it would be just being able to wake up and think I have, actually, woken up. To think "What have I got to do this day?". If I had that thought it would be something. I feel that if you say this to people they think you are being dramatic or something. I would if someone said it to me.'
TH: 'That's just how things are for you at the moment. Now being on 0, how do you cope?'
CL: 'By not caring about what's going on. Switching off. I drink from first thing in the morning. I don't eat. I'm taking tablets, it numbs me. I can sit and stare into space. I'm drinking more and more.'
TH: 'But not today.'
CL: 'I had no alcohol left. I will have to get some.'
TH: 'So you have none, it is not there and you can cope with this?'
CL: 'I knew I was coming here. So I will get some. First I will have to get rid of my father.'
TH: 'What else? Not thinking, not caring, what else gets you from one end of the day to the other?'
CL: 'That's just about it I think. I just don't care, I suppose, and also I know that I am going back abroad in eight weeks' time.'
TH: 'When you go back to your friends, out there, how will they know that somehow you have begun to sort something out? How would they know; they have not seen you for three months.'
CL: 'I would be more polite to them. I told everyone to get lost in no uncertain terms. I don't remember. I am amazed that I have so many good friends. They all stuck by me. I was rude and nasty to every single one. They would notice I would be strong and enthusiastic, not so down, turning hot and cold on them. One of

them really spoke to me about how I was. They treated me like a piece of glass, frightened I would start. They would not let me be alone. They would not speak to me about it.'

TH: 'Would you prefer them to be more open?'

CL: 'I would like to know what happened. I only know bits and pieces. I just woke up and I'd been in hospital for three weeks. Friends said what had happened, I could not remember anything.'

TH: 'It sounds like you have some good friends. What is it about you they want to know and care about?'

CL: (Laughs) 'I have no idea. I am surprised they do.'

TH: 'Because of what's happened but what would they say?'

CL: 'I would think it's my personality, I guess, because I have tried to help people and I was a decent person. I have always put on a front, made jokes, I was always covering what I really feel. You are "a good laugh", you just act. I would like to think I am a caring person – or was.'

TH: 'On a scale of 0 to 10, 0 is where you will just hope and pray this will go away and 10 is where you will do anything for it to go away, where are you?'

CL: '10.'

TH: 'During the next eight weeks would you be prepared to, at least, work with me here and try to find some answers?'

CL: 'Yes.'

TH: 'Before I take a break and discuss this with my colleagues, have I missed anything?'

CL: 'Can I just ask, will I get help? I mean will I get some therapy that helps me not just go away and take this pill or something?'

TH: 'That is what we are trying to find out, if we can work together to work this out. Exploring how we can find some new beginning to build on. My immediate answer is, "Yes, you will get some therapy and I would like to continue to see you to get you off 0, and move up the scale". That is the best thing I can say. We want to help, it's a collaboration.'

CL: 'Oh yes, but what I am trying to say, am I going to get some kind of therapy to try and help or go home and spend eight weeks on tranquillizers?'

TH: 'My reaction is, no, you'll get therapy here. What form that will take I'll discuss with my colleagues, and I'll take a break now if you'd like to get yourself a cup of tea? Is that OK?'

CL: 'Yes fine. We will continue and talk about this.'

BREAK

Message

TH: 'I think a great deal when I take a break and I have written it all down. I'd like to thank you for coming along, so we can begin to understand. Things are tough at the moment and coping from day to day is an effort. It sounds very frustrating to want your life different but not knowing what to do. Feeling depressed, by its very nature, makes taking the first steps difficult. What's clear is that you really want to work on finding solutions. And so we would like to see you again. Let me explain about the therapies on offer here, you have a place at the day hospital for the group programme, or see me here on an individual basis, or both. What do you think would suit you best?'

CL: 'What do you think?'

TH: 'In an eight-week period I think this would be better as it can be a lot more focused.'

CL: 'Then I would prefer this.'

TH: 'That's fine, I would like to see you at the beginning of next week' (Arranges time and date four days later).
So the last bit is this message, Theresa. In our experience, people often underestimate the strengths they have so we would like you to pay attention to everything you do, apart from drinking, that will help you to get through that day. We will talk about what helps you to get through next time.'

CL: 'Thank you, that gives me some hope at last! It feels like I have been running around in a state, you know ringing the helplines screaming, "Please will you tell me something that will make me want to live", and finally I'll be getting some help, thank you.'

Comments

This session represents the use of the model with multiple problems including self harm. The therapist's pace is slow and he uses indirect compliments only with Theresa to match how serious the situation is for her. She has a list of difficulties and the therapist resists the temptation to become an 'expert' by picking any single difficulty as more worthy of attention than another. Instead he concentrates on the Miracle Question (which is only partially answered), and future-oriented questions to get a picture of how things will be different for Theresa in the future. These are often answered by further descriptions of the problem or by her not being able to identify a clear miracle but the therapist sees this as simply an indication of how difficult things are for her at the present time. The therapist ignores the temptation to be an 'expert' again when Theresa talks about 'fear of going out'. With so many labels attached to this lady it was tempting to say, 'You mean agoraphobia', and through such language, diagnoses are born. There is no clear focus throughout the session but there are exceptions; three months ago things were better and Theresa is not sure how. She has also resisted the urge to harm herself and to drink today. She wants to be 'calmer' and has kept her friends and she wants the 'will to live'. She wants to return to work. The therapist uses the scaling questions to introduce the idea of small changes. Thus, the initial 'one step up the scale' is not left at 'I would wake up and want to live' but the therapist asks, 'What if wanting was a little bit later on, higher up the scale', making room for smaller changes to occur.

The task is asking Theresa to focus on anything that helps her get through the day and so is not concrete, but instead asks her to focus on times when she is 'up' and coping, and how come. The effect is to allow Theresa some hope while not taking on an 'expert role' and answering her questions or becoming the guru that will tell her how to want to live. Theresa is involved in the decision about what therapy she can receive and although she defers to the therapist it is the involvement at every stage of the session that makes this model one of empowerment. Suicide, depression, obsessions and alcoholism are all brought by the client but have little to do with her goals and it is these goals that the therapist focuses on. This allows the client and therapist to work in collaboration at finding solutions without the client feeling blamed or crazy, things are difficult but not impossible. Theresa began to present some complex ideas in the session such as, 'Others would see this as dramatic' and 'Solving one problem leads to another'. As mentioned earlier, if the therapist does not hypothesize and focuses on what the client wants then the client will hypothesize to the therapist and this, in our opinion, is a preferable state of affairs. Complex 'insight based' interpretations by the client of their own situation are a side effect of this model and counter some ideas that it is limited in the emotional or internal effect it has on clients. The overall effect is one of hope for the client even if the therapist still hasn't got a clear picture or clear answers to the questions in the session, sometimes that may take more time.

Session 2

Four days later the therapist and Theresa met again for the next session.

TH: 'So, it's been four days. So what's better?'
CL: 'I've felt a bit better over the weekend. I have not gone down so many times.'

TH: 'What were you doing that was different? On each day?'

CL: 'Nothing. I did not change anything since my week out of hospital. I don't know whether it's the tablets, or coming here.'

TH: 'They helped, you think?'

CL: 'Maybe that's what helped. It may be that I am thinking clearer, thinking why I got in this mess. I think it has been coming on for years. It's not something that suddenly occurred. I do not know what is contributing to me having a clearer mind.'

TH: 'Sometimes changes happen. You went away on Thursday feeling brighter?'

CL: 'Not really brighter – it was a relief. I did not know if it was going to help. Thursday evening is vague. It is getting better but everything is vague. There are points where I just go down but I do not stay down for hours now, I come up. Yesterday I went down for a while and wanted to kill myself.'

TH: 'How did you resist?'

CL: 'I cried a lot and got it out of my system. It tends to help.'

TH: 'On a scale of 0 to 10, when 10 is where you want to be, where would you say you are?'

CL: 'Maybe 3. Maybe I have accepted the fact that I had to come back to you and in the back of my mind this is not going to be forever.'

TH: 'If changes continue in the same way, with hope building over the next eight weeks, what do you expect to be different?'

CL: 'Being more in control of everything going on round me and myself. I feel bad about things I have done because I cannot control my temper, etc. Being in control of my situation.'

TH: 'How would someone else know?'

CL: 'I'd be more mellow. I'm up and down all day, doing wild, crazy things. I would be more in control of myself.'

TH: 'What else would you see?'

CL: 'Just being able to think clearly. I hope that would show itself. The main thing is to be more mellow, personally.'

TH: 'So you would notice a lot of changes in you? What about the way you lived your life? What would you like to be doing with your life?'

CL: 'I have to change, not work so much. I think this is the problem. I worry about it constantly, but I live for my work.'

TH: 'If we went along that road and you took a couple of steps away from work, bringing other things into your life, what other things would they be?'

CL: 'Being more sociable, having a hobby, which I am trying to do. Hospital gave you art work and now I am trying to keep busy with things just to keep it up.'

TH: 'You are doing that now?'

CL: 'I'm just wanting to do more craft work and try to concentrate but I don't have much concentration any more. I am worried about being away from work. I am reading books for pleasure. It is difficult to concentrate but I am trying to do something else.'

TH: 'Bringing some enjoyment into your life is hard work but it helps?'

CL: 'I do not think craft work helps at all – embroidery – maybe it does help. I still have problems which I don't know how to deal with. It is only when I understand how to deal with these, things may change but it is difficult.'

TH: 'In eight weeks' time will you expect to know how to deal with this?'

CL: 'It is worse being here. If I am trying to pull myself together here it is harder – it is better to be away from the family and do it.'

TH: 'So these 12 weeks are a real challenge. Any changes you make will be a real achievement.'

CL: 'Yes. Oh the other thing is that over the weekend, I have not been eating. This helped.'

TH: 'How does not eating help?'

CL: 'It makes me feel better. I think it is going into the foreground. Definitely this was a contributing factor to my feeling better.'

TH: 'In an ideal world, would you like this out of your life?'

CL: 'I don't think it will ever go. I don't think you can cure it, you can put it in the background maybe. For five or six years I have had it.'

TH: 'You think you can control it but not get over it?'

CL: 'Yes.'

TH: 'There is a lot going on; preoccupation with work, in the background for a long time are the eating problems, and you are over here. If you could sort out one of these problems which one would you sort out first?'

CL: 'Depression – but I don't know if you can. I think I only live for my work, anything else that goes on in my life is not important.'

TH: 'Would you like this to be different?'

CL: 'Yes, but I don't think I will get any better until I get a balance.'

TH: 'You have begun to make a small change. Six months ago work was 100 per cent of your life but now you are reading and doing craft work. If six months ago it was 100 per cent, what ratio is it, work to leisure, now?'

CL: 'I do not think I can cope with anything at the moment so it's hard to say.'

TH: 'What do you think will be a good balance?'

CL: 'Sixty per cent work, 40 per cent social, even 70–30 per cent would be better than nothing.'

TH: 'You have taken a small step. What more do you think you could bring into your life, social activities, etc.?'

CL: 'I really enjoy art, opera, ballet. I could try to introduce these things into my life. If I went back now I would go straight back into my work. I realize now I have been depressed for years. It was becoming more difficult to be engaged in the work as well.'

TH: 'If you went back to work would it be 100 per cent of your life, dominating your time?'

CL: 'That would be kind of pointless. At the moment I think it would dominate still.'

TH: 'Do you think your chances of leading a healthy lifestyle will improve, if in the eight weeks here you could alter the balance now, so the more you use these eight weeks to get your life in order, you can carry on when you go back to your position abroad.'

CL: 'Definitely. The main thing I want to get rid of is wanting to commit suicide. This is the main thing.'

TH: 'So you're saying you want to find more things satisfactory and meaningful in your life. As you introduce new activities that will give you a purpose to go on with your life rather than end it.'

CL: 'Maybe then I'll be just getting on with my life. Maybe I try to block out the fact that I have to wait eight weeks until. . . . Yesterday I wanted to go back. I would get a plane back and that would be it. I am afraid of that part when I take the knife to myself and cannot remember anything about it. I will just walk in and get a plane ticket one day, I am afraid of that. That would be like taking a step in the past.'

TH: 'When you are feeling desperate, as you do, any change that moves you forward is helpful. When you are in that position you will naturally take the easiest way. Although not eating is not a good thing if it helps you to move forward so you will be stronger and don't need to harm yourself, perhaps at the moment it is important to move in the right direction, forward.'

CL: 'I cannot cope with five difficult things at once. I am trying to get over depression. I don't bother to eat.'

TH: 'Are you saying you are just missing meals or that you are starving yourself?'

CL: 'I'm starving myself. It has got worse.'

TH: 'You know that as you are able to get stronger in one area you will deal with others. Strength spreads around.'

CL: 'But also if you are starving yourself, you are starving your brain.'

TH: 'Yes. Although you have taken a step forward and beginning to feel stronger, one of the things that has helped you, is that you stopped eating, but if you continue, physically, you will not be able to go on to think clearly. I guess you'll have to find a balance.'

CL: 'Is that a subconscious way to commit suicide? Maybe this is how I have mellowed.'

TH: 'What would it take for you to begin to eat just enough to get by each day?'

CL: 'At the moment I don't think about it. I do not want to eat.'

TH: 'Even though you don't want to, what would it take for you to not want to but say, "I am going to".'

CL: 'I will become extremely depressed again. This must be a factor. If someone made me eat I would not.'

TH: 'What if you told yourself that you have to make this balance?'

CL: 'I would have to want to do it. I would have to have the will to do it.'

TH: 'What if at first you do not want to eat but you do it, and it's only a little bit up the road it turns into a want?'

CL: 'I would have to eat. What about the fact I was eating in hospital and when I came out I was very depressed.'

TH: 'Over the weekend you stopped eating and you felt better. You seem to connect the two. What if it was coincidence and that you were doing something else as well that helped you; what if the eating and feeling better were not connected?'

CL: 'I'd have to eat to find out. I don't think it will do anything. I will try.'

TH: 'I guess you'll be prepared to find out whether it will work or not. You have been reading more and doing art. What would it take for you to do more so that it takes over more of your time?'

CL: 'That it would be easier – to take on more arts and crafts and doing this for pleasure. Because I have no choice now, it was always my work, it seems everything I need to do with the research is at the University, computers and everything, and I do not want my friends to know I am here so I cannot do any work, so I have to do something else even though I don't want to. I am going into arts and things. This will take more of my time.'

TH: 'As you progress, bringing more pleasurable, social activities, does that include people?'

CL: 'That would be difficult as my tolerance level is low. I have friends over here and that would be important to some extent but I have more friends abroad.'

TH: 'When would you know your tolerance level was sufficient?'

CL: 'When I did not holler.'

TH: 'How would you know you have reached that level until you are in the situation? At 3, how would you know that you have moved to 3 and a half?'

CL: 'If I eat on the day and it was not so bad or if I wake in the morning and do not want to suffocate myself. Over the weekend I was numb. But I did not want to kill myself.'

TH: 'At three and a half that numbness would change into getting up and coping with the day? How would you know when you have moved up a full point?'

CL: 'Consistency and just wanting more. Saying to myself, "I will do this", and getting up to do art or see a performance.'

TH: 'What works best for you? Do you wake up and fill your day or do you plan the evening before?'

CL: 'I don't plan it. To some extent I am doing this today, but that's it.'

TH: 'Would it be difficult if you programmed for the day?'

CL: 'Maybe it would help rather than just getting up and thinking I have got to do this. I know I am doing this but what do I do until then? To have some control over what I am doing.'

TH: 'Have I missed anything?'

CL: 'I would like to ask you, being here is bringing me to a problem that was removed when I was abroad. How, at the same time, can I try and get well and be in the situation which caused me to be ill in the first place?'

TH: 'It will take a lot of hard effort. There is, now, a glimmer of hope. Your aim sounds like it is to make a purpose in your life, not just work. You want a balance to your life, then you can begin to respect yourself and feel good about yourself, and if you are feeling good then you can begin to take on challenges with confidence. If you can achieve what you want to achieve, over here, then you can transfer that.'

CL: 'Won't it be harder for me here?'

TH: 'Yes, you cannot get away from it. Then it will be more than an achievement.'

CL: 'I ran away before from all this, I put myself into work.'

BREAK

Message

TH: 'You are facing up to areas challenging to you and you are beginning to do something about them. You said, and I agree, that you cannot deal with that all at the same time. A small pebble in the pond affects all the pond. Change leads to change. If you know you've done the best you can in the area you want to face up to, that's all you can do.'

CL: 'What guarantees are there?'

TH: 'To be 9 or 10? I will work with you over the next eight weeks, it will be a lot of hard work. You will find you will take further steps with confidence, and then we can look at when you go back and look at resources there and what the next step will be.
I have been very impressed with you – how you can turn your life around and how you do things you want. You have begun to take the first small steps towards that. You have ideas how you can build on this; ballet, meeting friends. The last couple of days have been slightly better. You think this is because not eating leads to feeling better. I wonder if that is coincidence; that it is unrelated? You have not found out what made you feel better.'
CL: 'Even though I had anorexia in the past, and I feel better not to eat?'
TH: 'That might be true in this case.'
CL: 'This will be very hard work. I'll have to eat to find out.'
TH: 'With a lot of effort, determination and strength you have done something difficult. A little each day, that might help you even more realize what you are capable of. I want you to notice what helps you to get on more and more.'
CL: 'The planning each day will help. I am thinking that now. It will, definitely, help me.'

Comments

Again, changes are small but may be due to Theresa not eating. While this may be seen as something preferable to taking a knife to herself or the family in the short term, while she makes other changes, it is clearly not an 'exception' that the therapist can support. The therapist invites Theresa to question her 'either/or frame' (either I starve myself or I feel depressed) by introducing other variables. Perhaps it is coincidence that she has stopped eating and feels better, perhaps there are some other reasons why she feels better that she has not noticed? Logically, this is possible and as Theresa points out she may have to eat to discover if it was not eating that made her feel positive, or if it was the drugs or the sessions of therapy or something else. Rather than forcing Theresa to eat (which she says wouldn't work anyway) asking her to do what she is good at (experimenting and researching a topic as she does for a profession) opens up possibilities for her and allows her to eat without feeling she is losing face or being forced into it. 'Deconstruction', as discussed earlier, can be therapeutically used to challenge a concrete idea. In this case, as a logical question, the therapist explores whether or not eating will help Theresa. This leads to Theresa actually deconstructing her own idea by saying, 'but if I starve myself I am also starving my brain and I won't think clearly'. Since her goal is to think clearly this would not make sense. Interestingly, rather than the therapist's questions 'colluding' with Theresa not eating (by asking how does this help or stating that a small move forward may be necessary by such means in the short term, to stop her taking a knife to people), his being prepared to see *if* it helps and how come, or if the risks outweigh the benefits, invited the client to come up with alternatives to behaviour. Ownership of such alternatives is then with the *client* not the therapist, preventing loss of face and encouraging experiment. Also the difficulty then becomes a logical one; if Theresa wants to think clearly then what can she do to achieve this, given that starving herself does not help her reach this goal?

The idea that you have to want to eat in order to eat enough to get you through the day is challenged by a question, 'What if that is a little further down the line from now, what can you do while you are waiting to want to eat, what will help you move one step forward?'. Theresa has achieved a lot in her academic and work career and some of this has been by initially doing things she may not have wanted to do. This is a truism for all of us and an example of the fact that skills and experiences from other areas may be used by clients on their complaint. For example, crafts and art take control, concentration, patience and confidence as well as skill and application. These skills may transfer to Theresa's ability to control her up and down moods, to remember things, to feel more aware and alive and to be creatively absorbed instead of 'numb'. Linking clients to discipline, application, skills and fun they had in other areas may help them to value and use these experiences in their present situation.

The same task is used to notice what helps, since that shifted Theresa a little and also matched the fact that she still feels out of control and vague about what helped. A concrete task may not have helped her at this stage.

Sessions 3 to 8

It took some time, until session four, for Theresa to begin to focus on research skills that she naturally possessed and to see the time between the sessions as an opportunity to research her life and what worked for her. She began to feel that it was herself that made her feel better or worse by how she focused on the difficulty. She began to do more planning of her days and as result used her interest in art and began to mix again. She continued to introduce planning for each day and being active and was less sure about the eating/unhappiness 'either/or' set she had created. As this occurred she became calmer at home and approached her parents differently in a way that allowed them to trust her more and so she got more privacy. She was no longer suicidal by session six and returned to her work by session eight stating she was calmer and more stable. She remained interested in hobbies, as well as work, and saw the leisure time as a part of allowing her to work to her best and in this change of viewing of the problem was able to allow herself more fun. Since her return, she sends the therapist a postcard from time to time recording any further progress. There has not been another suicide attempt or allied problem for over two years.

The sessions with Client B are examples of follow-up sessions. The client covers a lot of material and is allowed to tell her story but the therapist concentrates on focusing her on, 'What will help?'.

Case example 2

Sharon is a young, single woman referred to our clinic by a psychiatrist, having a long established pattern of cutting. She had previous counselling interventions which had not made any significant impact on her behaviour. She went on over a series of sessions to stop the cutting previously.

Learning outcomes

What is most apparent over the sessions is the absence of a concept of relapse; behaviours which could be seen as negative are explored in the light of how the client coped with them, learnt how to stop, how they 'cut back on talk', etc. Other areas of behaviour are only explored in as much as they throw up positive behaviours which reflect on the client's goals.

Session 1

TH: 'How are things. What's better?'
CL: 'Nothing. Two weeks ago I crashed my car. Dad had a go. I have not spoken to him since.'
TH: 'You have stuck to your guns?'
CL: 'It's a nightmare.'
TH: 'How have you been?'
CL: 'Bloody miserable, really got me down.'
TH: 'How have you coped with your dad confronting you and not speaking to him? It's been hard on you?'

CL: 'I was all right after the car crash, all right about the accident, then I spoke to mum and asked about the damage. A bloke came round and said it would be no more than £900. Dad went mad. I said this was my problem but he started having a go at me. Mum came in arguing. I went to talk to her to explain, but she didn't want to know. Then we had a heart-to-heart. I cannot be bothered to speak to him, he makes me sick, drives me mad. I know it sounds silly but I am going to try and find somewhere else to live.'

TH: 'You decided you are going to move and you cut yourself once this time?'

CL: 'Yes. Just the once but it's cleared up now.'

TH: 'Was it as bad as you've done before?'

CL: 'Worse than last time.'

TH: 'How did you stop yourself?'

CL: 'I don't know. Felt like I'd done enough.'

TH: 'You felt like you'd done enough and then you stopped? You had a really difficult time, you cut yourself once and you made a decision about moving out.'

CL: 'Yes.'

TH: 'You are going to do what you decided and your mum agrees with that and you have stuck to your guns about the car. What else?'

CL: 'That's it really.'

TH: 'Have there been any other changes, times that you felt like hurting yourself and you have managed not to?'

CL: 'I don't think so.'

TH: 'So, apart from that, you survived? It sounds that this week has been really tough and, somehow, you have got through. What have you learnt?'

CL: 'I think I can cope with this. It was my fault. My friend fainted. I went mental. My other friend was all right and the bloke I hit was really all right, I was expecting him to be killed. I was thinking that I could have killed these people but they said nobody was hurt. Then I was thinking about my car. I just went mental about it. I was hysterical. My friend was kicking the door to get out of the car. I thought it was going to explode. He said, "The look on your face when I was kicking the door!", I thought I was taking it really well.'

TH: 'So you got your car back and someone came round to look at the damage. Out of all that disaster you were able to cut yourself just the once and that was when you argued with your dad.'

CL: 'If something had happened to one of my friends I don't know what I'd have done.'

TH: 'But your dad got to you the way the car didn't.'
CL: 'Yes, but I am going to leave.'
TH: 'How will that help?'
CL: 'Just to get away from him. I know I am not perfect but being away from him will help a lot better. I cannot do this until May anyway. I'm paying £80 a month for the car and now £45 a month to pay off the loan.'
TH: 'What do you think the next little step will be so that you can say "I can cope with this better". What will the next step be?'
CL: 'I'd have to take it bit by bit. I don't feel so bad at the moment. If I can get my car back I will be all right.'
TH: 'Really, can it be fixed?'
CL: 'Yes.'
TH: 'Since then you had a row with dad, scraped your arm a bit worse than last time, although you stopped. What's it been like since then? Have you been sorting out the car, hatching plans for moving out, grabbing some work, or what have you been doing?'
CL: 'Grabbing some work. Been out the last two Tuesdays. I felt really bad. The first Tuesday I was very depressed but the boys cheered me up.'
TH: 'And they managed to pull you out of it and you let yourself be pulled out of it?'
CL: 'I wanted to. Tuesday I went out and started getting this bloody cold.'
TH: 'How are you going to keep this going?'
CL: 'No point in talking about the weeks ahead. Maybe just think two minutes beforehand what I am going to do.'
TH: 'And your aim is three weeks? Still three without cutting at all? You nearly made it this time. Do you think your chances are better of making three weeks the less you argue with your dad?'
CL: 'If we had not had that row it would have been all right unless something else happened. I don't know. If we had not had a row I think it would have been all right. Something else happened. Bit fed up.'
TH: 'All right, so by not rowing with dad you increase the chances that you are not going to cut yourself. You are coping with the car crash without harming yourself.'
CL: 'I could have killed myself, got depressed about it.'
TH: 'That's how it goes.'
CL: 'I don't want to go through that again.'
TH: 'Do you think things will keep on track if you do not argue with your dad?'
CL: 'Yes, and mum.'

TH: 'Keep going to work, take each day at a time. A lot has happened. Do you think I have missed anything? Is there anything more you want to talk about? Are you happy with this session?'

CL: 'As happy as I can be.'

BREAK

Message

TH: 'I'm very impressed, it has been a really tough week and anybody would have been upset. All this with the car crash and dad, you have only managed to cut yourself once. We think this is really good. You are changing, you look different to us. It's clearly evident you are wanting to make changes and have worked very hard and are quite capable of getting better. We like the idea of you keeping out of your parents' hair and standing up for yourself. Keep noticing all the things that move you a little closer to how you want to be so we can talk about it next time.'

Session 2

TH: 'What happened?'

CL: 'The beginning of the week was a nightmare. The rest wasn't too bad.'

TH: 'The first two weeks were OK?'

CL: 'No problems.'

TH: 'The beginning of this week was bad. How did you cope? What did you do?'

CL: 'Injured myself a little bit. Scratched myself with some scissors.'

TH: 'How did you stop?'

CL: 'I got fed up I think. I didn't try hard enough to make an impression.'

TH: 'Did you stop quicker than before?'

CL: 'I was worried about work.'

TH: 'How did you cope with that?'

CL: 'I'm still worried. The man who knows everything about the section is leaving a week on Wednesday. I panicked. I thought I was going to have a lot of responsibility, I was worried and annoyed. He did not tell me. I'm not that confident, if I have any problems I ask him. If I cannot do something I am completely stuck. I will get the blame for it. I was really upset.'

TH: 'And that was worse on Monday?'

CL: 'Yes. I felt I couldn't cope but I talked it through with the manager and then felt a little better.'

TH: 'How did you know that was the right thing to do?'
CL: 'I don't know, but he made me feel a lot more confident.'
TH: 'So you had a real shock about someone important leaving. You talked it through, settled down and, somehow, you found it more difficult to cut. How did you do that?'
CL: 'Well, I just couldn't be bothered to go through with it.'
TH: 'You've been bothered on other occasions. How did it go right?'
CL: 'I'm not sure' (puzzled).

Note how the therapist, despite the difficulties and setbacks of the previous weeks, focused on the area of improvement and 'What helps' but goes with the client at her own pace.

In the second session the therapist is careful to credit the client with the improvements; 'positive blame' as de Shazer puts it, rather than leaving it as chance or apathy.

Case example 3

Alan is a young single man with psychotic symptoms. He was concerned about the way the voices interfered with his life. The example shows that the presence of psychotic symptoms in themselves are no bar to using these techniques.

Learning outcomes

In this example, the therapist, rather than using the Miracle Question *per se*, painstakingly builds up a picture of what the client wants by asking him how he would like things to be, and how he, the therapist, can help him.

In the session with a psychotic client, the therapist focused on 'What helps?' to cut through the confusing material so that the client can build a solid bridge into how he would like the future to be.

CL: 'Mum was getting concerned, I was in trouble with the police again. I was drinking but not drinking every day. I haven't come to terms that I have got a problem. Something must be wrong in my mind. I cannot come to terms with the problems. Indoors, the other day, I broke down with my mum. She said, "Tell me what the problem is". My sister had a baby, she is two now. Sometimes when I am holding the baby, I love her a lot, I have the baby in my arms, I wouldn't hurt her but I sometimes hear a voice say, "Drop her on her head". I have to give her back. I put her on the floor or give her back to my mum or sister and I have to go into my bedroom; I start walking round the bedroom. I wonder why I think these things. When I am in the street I see people staring at me and I go up to them and say, "What are you fucking looking at?". I think they are trying to do something to me. On the station platform I kick their legs and trip them up, I hear something telling me to do something sometimes. I tell myself there's nothing happening, it just comes through like the voice.'

TH: 'Somehow you are managing not to drink every day?'

CL: 'Sometimes I don't drink for months on end. The other weekend I just went out, I was scared, I started drinking. When I get in this position I get worried, scared. It becomes too much. Everything gets too much, loads of confusion, just go and drink and stop taking my tablets. I've started taking them again now.'

TH: 'Taking them, do they help?'

CL: 'They calm everything down. Sometimes I wake up, I think about life, what am I doing here; I think I am here for some sort of purpose but get confused what I am supposed to be doing. Sometimes I wake up and I will be fine. I see something on television about firemen or gardening and I think I will be a gardener or a fireman; I have a conversation about being a gardener or fireman or being a pilot. It gets very confusing. I only do this when I am by myself, not when anyone else is in the room.'

TH: 'So when there are other people around?'

CL: 'I don't do it.'

TH: 'You don't get so confused?'

CL: 'No, I just sit there and think thoughts that I am something else, have a conversation with someone who isn't there about the World Cup, Ryan Giggs. I have a laugh and a few drinks with him but I know he is not there. Have a laugh and joke, I know he is not there but I am still doing it. The other month I went to an acting school. I wanted to be an actor but now I don't.'

TH: 'What changed your mind?'

CL: 'I was watching telly, watching films, I thought I could be an actor, went up to London, convinced I was an actor, an actor taking acting lessons. Woke up one day and thought I don't want to be an actor, I paid £600. Waste of money.'

TH: 'How do you hope we can help you and what would you like us to help you with?'

CL: 'I don't know, that's why I am here. Find out what's wrong. I find it hard. If I had a leg missing I could understand that, obviously, I can't run. But because I am a physically fit person, I find it hard to come to terms that something is wrong with me.'

TH: 'So you got an idea that coming to terms with the fact that there is something wrong with you might help you?'

CL: 'I think it would make life less confusing.'

TH: 'OK, and you want your life to be a bit simpler?

CL: 'Yes. I want to serve some sort of purpose. It gets confusing. Even though I have got my parents. I have had girlfriends. I can be going out with a girl but I think she is planning to do something to me so I stop seeing her. It gets very lonely.'

TH: 'So you start relationships OK but then you stop?'

CL: 'No reason at all I start having arguments with them and she won't know what I am arguing about and she will be totally confused. She has not done anything. I have made this up and start rowing.'

TH: 'Why would you want to do this?'

CL: 'I would just be sitting there talking and I would say, "Who did you go out with last night", and she would say, "I did not go out last night" and I would say, "Yes you fucking did, you did go out last night" you know, and I just get convinced that she did go out last night and would not want to see her. I think she is lying to me but she is not and I cannot come to terms with that, I make up my mind. It's puzzling what is going on, why do I think these things?'

TH: 'So if you could find out what was going on how would you think your life would be different? How would you like it to be different if you understood these things?'

CL: 'It would make life much simpler, normal. I don't know what normal is. Just get out and do everyday things, go to work. I had a job a few months ago now, working in a garage, it lasted about eight hours. I was asked to leave, I could not deal with the public. I started throwing things at them, smashing them in the face. I said to the girl who got me the job – I've known her years, she lived down the street – I said to her I cannot work here, it would not be fair to you, you got me the job here, I'm no good, just eight hours and I left. I would like to get a proper job. I'm hoping to get a bricklaying course. That would be good, help to take my mind off it.'

TH: 'OK, so you have decided to do bricklaying, you think it might take your mind off it?'

CL: 'At the moment, bricklaying.'

TH: 'What makes you think you can stick to that?'

CL: 'Just an idea, I have asked the DSS to put me on the course.'

TH: 'So you try all these things but it is hard for you to stick at them and you find yourself arguing with all these people, it gets you into trouble with the police, and you have a drink to calm you down.'

CL: 'I just sort of like . . . my parents go to work, come home, go out with friends, go shopping. Some days I won't go out of the house. I just sit in the corner of a room listening to music or the telly. I have to hear a word I like on the telly then I turn the telly off, like "love", or if I hear a word like "kill" I cannot turn the telly off. Sometimes when I start thinking or getting confused, thoughts run all through my head, I put the telly and music on so there is loads of noise and it drowns it out, all the noises in my head and all the feelings, so I just sit there. It is strange.'

TH: 'So part of you would like to understand these things a bit more.'

CL: 'Yes. To find out why it is happening. Even when I was younger I had this problem but I never talked about it, I like to keep things to myself. It's hard to trust someone, they will tell someone else then everyone will know something is wrong. So I always keep things close to myself, even when I was younger. I just broke down the other night indoors, on my knees crying. I used to go out on the lorry with my dad but when he changed gear there was a noise, "shshshshsh". When I was ten, every time I heard this noise I thought my dad was throwing something at me in the lorry and I used to turn round and look at him but he would still be driving. I was convinced that every time I had heard this noise he was throwing something at me. I am 24 now, like 12 years I have not told anybody about this but it has always been there and I have to understand why. Strange.'

TH: 'And you would like to understand these things a bit more, and you would like your life to be a bit simpler so that you do not think too deeply about stuff like this?'

CL: 'I only keep these things to myself. Tablets calm me down. I think they have.'

TH: 'Remembering the lorry, this seemed quite important?

CL: 'Yes. Like one of the things I remember when I started getting these thoughts – sometimes when I am in the house on my own, I sometimes do it now, going back to an empty house, I pull a piece of hair out and put it over the door so that when I come back if the hair has gone I know someone has gone in. I know normal people don't do this.'

TH: 'And how do you think normal people will deal with anxieties about going back to an empty house or when they think people are looking at them, how do you imagine normal people would deal with these worries?'

CL: 'It is not the fear of going back to an empty house, it's whether someone is inside the house. You know, I think someone got in so I put a piece of hair over the door, and if it's gone I know someone came in and I run round the house checking behind chairs making sure no one is there. Sometimes I do it now, not all the time, I look in the cupboards in the loft. Sometimes, not all the time.'

TH: 'So you get an idea that it links back, it reminds you of the things that people do in childhood, that people do to check places.'

CL: 'You move on, get friends, get a girlfriend, drift away from friends when you start a relationship. I have been out with some right nice girls but I just start rowing with them for no reason at all. I think they are out to do something, make up lots of shit. I think I have got stuck in childhood.'

TH: 'So you have got an idea that some how you are stuck with some of the things you could not let go of earlier in your life? What kind of things would you like to let go of now?'

CL: 'I don't know, strange thoughts.'

TH: 'What would you prefer to be doing with these thoughts. Everybody has weird thoughts from time to time, what would you like to be doing with them?'

CL: 'Don't know. Focusing on some sort of energy.'

TH: 'What about your life at the minute, what do you think you are doing right?'

CL: 'I think this is right at the moment, talking. Mum said try and get yourself sorted out. I'd like to cut the top of my head off and look inside and find out what is going on and put it back in the right place. I think I am 24, I feel much younger inside. I think, "Why am I here?", "What is my purpose in life?". Maybe there might not be a purpose you just do what you do. Maybe I am still a little kid.'

TH: 'Does that idea help? What helps more, purpose in life and you have to find it or an idea you just do what you have to do in life? What is the nicer idea? What do you prefer?'

CL: 'Just doing what you have to do. I am put here for some sort of reason. Sometimes I have been out in the street just walking, I think I am invisible, even now I am talking daft but it just happens. It has took a lot to come down here and talk about it, just talk about it to myself and try and solve the problems myself, but I end up going out and getting drunk. Just escape.'

TH: 'So you got your imagination very well developed and when you walk along you can get very deep into stuff and imagine stuff and you would like to have that more under control and take life as it is?'

CL: 'Get on with everyday life.'

TH: 'On a scale of 0 to 10, where 0 is the worst you have ever felt and 10 would be exactly how you would like your life to be, where would you be today on that scale?'

CL: '5, I suppose.'

TH: 'Half way, what small thing would bring you up to 6? What would be the first steps that would tell you have a handle on these things? The first thing you would like to tackle?'

CL: 'Get up in the morning and not think, just think, "What I am going to have for breakfast?", not what is going to happen to me for the rest of my life. Just take each minute as it comes. Don't put ten years in five minutes.'

TH: 'You think you are looking at a big picture that makes everything confusing, you would like to get up in the morning and not think, just think, "What am I going to have for breakfast?" and the next step after that and the next step after that, just break it up into small bits. What else would help you move along a little bit? You are on tablets and that has helped and already you are on 5. I am very impressed that you are able to decide what is imaginary and what is real. This is important and I am impressed that when you have got the baby and your imagination tells you to drop it on its head, you hand it back to its mum, you go away and give yourself a bit of time to get it together. That is important.'

CL: 'Living at home with my parents I have their support, if I was on my own I might have done something quite drastic by now. I have thought, at times, of killing myself. Just get out when things are getting on top of me, get drunk and think of killing myself. When I used to drive my car – I don't drive anymore – be driving along and a voice would tell me to pull the steering wheel down and ram the car.'

TH: 'So, having other people around, and the help and support of your family helps you to decide what is imaginary and what is real? Helps you not to give way to all this your mind says to you?'

CL: 'I think having responsibility as well would help. If I could take a job.'

TH: 'That sounds like a big step. What would be the first move towards getting a job you can stick to?'

CL: 'Getting over the anxieties that people will try and do things to me all the time. Trust. I find it hard to trust people, find it hard to trust myself and this is the first person you have to learn to trust.'

TH: 'You would like to trust people more?'

CL: 'Self trust. I read a lot as well to try and find out what is wrong. Try and solve problems, read about mental illness, what's my problem. I find it hard to talk to people like doctors.'

TH: 'You think reading about it does not help you?'

CL: 'No.'

TH: 'You would like to take one day at a time, in smaller steps, not looking at the bigger picture, what you are going to do in twenty years' time? You think the key to this is beginning to trust yourself more and give yourself credit for what you are doing well and be safe. Switch off these thoughts sometimes when you want to and if you can trust yourself a bit more you might be able to trust other people, which is the key to sticking to a job and moving forward to where you want to go.

What other small steps have you begun already on this journey? You have gone back on the tablets and that has helped, you have decided to come here, which is quite a thing to do to talk to people rather than bottle things up. What other things have you started to do to help?'

CL: 'Sometimes when I am indoors, my parents, they don't row, but when they have little arguments, I thought they were having arguments about me. I don't understand their relationship but I have come to terms now it is nothing to do with me.'

TH: 'How did you do that?'

CL: 'I just had a talk with my mum and she said, "Sometimes me and dad have a little argument".'

TH: 'You checked it out with your mum? She was able to let you know it was nothing to do with you?'

CL: 'It did not stem from me.'

TH: 'You are a man who takes responsibilities for the world's problems even when they are not your fault. What else would help? A bricklaying course is a nice idea to start with but you are quite realistic about it, you are not sure you know if you could stick it. Whether you stick it depends on how you trust other people, which is part of the other things you are sorting out yourself. What else would help?'

CL: 'I suppose trying not to worry about what everyone else is up to. I think that's a lot to do with it.'

TH: 'What thoughts would you have instead? What would you like to be thinking about instead?'

CL: 'I don't know. More positive things. If I am worrying about what everyone else is saying or doing it's a lot of wasted energy. Wasted energy thinking and worrying about everybody else's problems.'

TH: 'So, if you had to have positive thoughts, to replace these thoughts, what ones would you choose, what might you think about?'

CL: 'Making money.'

TH: 'You would like to think of ways to make money, to get your life stable, rather than thinking what other people are up to. Is there anything you would like to ask me or thought I should have asked you or might have missed, and you want to tell us?'

CL: 'When I was on probation, I was doing well. I was talking to the probation officer every two weeks. I suppose I lied in a way, saying I was feeling well, but I don't think I was.'

TH: 'So, for a while you got an idea that going to see someone, regularly, to just talk about these things helped. Just seeing your probation officer, you felt this helped? Anything else you wanted to check with us?'

CL: 'No.'

BREAK

Message

TH: 'It sounds that life can be very confusing and that your greatest wish is to live an ordinary life from minute to minute and not have these worrying thoughts in your head.

For next time, we would like you to notice anything that helps you to live life in an ordinary way, that helps with the worrying thoughts and gets you from 5 to 6.'

Note the question, 'How do you think normal people deal with anxieties', that developed out of the session and shows that even some psychotic clients have the capability to think and build and plan how they would like their life to be in a realistic way. The therapist is reluctant to accept large and unrealistic goals ('get a job') but tends to build slowly on the present exceptions and instances where the client can sort out or resist the upsetting ideas.

15

Research into Brief Therapy and Solution Focused Therapy

Learning objectives

By the end of the chapter the reader should be aware of some of the research into the area of Brief Therapy and Solution Focused Therapy in particular. New work from Gerry Brophy and Kenny Gouck in the Angus NHS Trust, Scotland, is also included with their permission. The reader should be able to question ideas that more therapy is a good thing, that Brief Therapy is necessarily superficial, that clients do not make change themselves, and that brevity in therapy belongs to any one particular school of thought since examples of research indicating brief outcomes are provided from solution focused, single session, brief focused, behavioural, and psychoanalytical perspectives.

For material in this chapter about Brief Therapy we are indebted to Koss and Butchers' seminal chapter from Garfield and Bergins, *Handbook of Psychotherapy and Behavioural Change* (1971, pp. 627–70), and direct the reader to this resource to discover further research summaries on the topic.

When less is not more

Practitioners are now (rightly) requested to base their approaches on research. This chapter draws together diverse material on Brief Therapies and may help the reader consider the research base behind the techniques described earlier in this book.

It is clear when taking an overview of the subject that there is still a need for further research into Solution Focused Therapy. For our own part, we have not entered the arena in any depth due to a lack of skills (we are innumerate) and a lack of resources (our attempts to access funds within our Trust for researchers were never successful). There still needs to be a full outcome study into Solution Focused Therapy using standard rating scales over an 18-month period, or longer, with a large group of clients in order to fully understand the model's effectiveness. However, we can not discount the work undertaken by de Shazer and his team (USA), Moshe Talmon (Israel), Diane Iveson (London), and Gerry Brophy and Kenny Gouck (Scotland). All of these pieces of work (independently undertaken), in some cases duplicating methodology, suggest an approximate 'success rate' of 70 per cent for the model. This places Solution Therapy in the 'about successful as anything else' band of therapies in general, and suggests that your choice of therapeutic stance is more about how you want to work rather than one approach being winner of the 'most successful talking therapy' award.

All clinicians make statistical claims that their approach is better than another and Solution Therapy needs more research before it can enter such a debate (if it sees such discussion as useful, that is). However, research into brief approaches in general does dispel a few myths about what works in therapy and how long successful therapy takes.

Garfield and Bergins' *Handbook of Psychotherapy and Behavioural Change* (1971) contains an excellent overview by Mary P. Koss (Kent State University) and James N. Butcher (University of Minnesota) of Brief Psychotherapy. They begin with a quote from Garfield himself

> It is now generally recognised that patients, when they enter psychological treatment do not anticipate that their program of treatment will be prolonged but believe that their problems will require a few sessions at most. Indeed, patients typically come to psychological treatment seeking specific and focal problem resolution, not for general personality 'overhauls' as assumed in the past.
>
> (Garfield, 1978, pp. 191–232)

Garfield goes on to say, 'Brief Therapy Methods, once thought to be appropriate only to less severe problems, have actually been shown to be effective with severe and chronic problems if treatment goals are kept reasonable', and, 'Brief treatment methods have generally the same success rate as longer term treatment programs'. He cites insurance companies and pre-paid health programs as exerting an influence on therapy by restricting the number of sessions and so encouraging practitioners to find briefer approaches.

From our own pilot programmes in primary health care, GP Fundholders certainly prefer to buy focused assessment and treatment packages for their clients that can be used in the surgery and have some effect within six sessions (Hunt *et al.*, 1994). There is much to attract GPs (and health purchasers in general) to brief therapy. It may save money and resources in the long run. For instance, Cummings and Follette supported the usefulness of short term interventions in reducing the overall utilization of medical services. Looking at a five-year period they concluded that one session of psychotherapy resulted in a significant reduction in a client's use of medical services. They summarized this by stating, 'The findings that one session only, with no repeat psychological visits, could reduce medical utilisation by 60 per cent over the following five years, was surprising and totally unexpected' (Cummings and Follette, 1976).

Solution Focused Therapy has proved ideal for this flexible assessment (with advice to the GP on re-referral if necessary, based on what the client wants from therapy) or brief treatment role (Hawkes, unpublished paper, 1997).

What is Brief Therapy?

Research into Brief Therapy is numerous and enlightening. As we have seen, Solution Focused Therapy is brief by outcome rather than design and despite de Shazer's interest in keeping the 'Brief' prefix in 'Brief Solution Focused Therapy' it does not feature in this book as essential (sorry Steve). Solution focused thinking does not *have* to be brief, we can even say that this is up to the client as well as the therapist. However, Solution Focused Therapy does seem to meet seven of nine 'technical characteristics that most brief treatments have in common' as described by Koss and Butcher (1971). They looked at brief therapy from psychoanalysis, behavioural and 'alternative' perspectives (Solution Focused Therapy would presumably be an 'alternative'), and found that they shared nine items:

1. promptness of intervention;
2. rapid early assessment;
3. quickly established interpersonal relationship;
4. limitation of therapeutic goals;
5. directive management of the sessions by the therapist (in so far as a map is used);
6. centring the therapeutic content around a focus;
7. flexibility in choice of technique.

The other two which do not necessarily correspond are:

1. Management of temporal limitation by therapists. This can be met by our usually sticking to an hour per session but we do not

set a firm target time and this is an innovation that Koss and Butcher may not have been aware of since their main comparison was between psychoanalytic and brief therapy and behavioural therapy at the time of the article.

2. Ventilation of catharsis. This happens in Solution Therapy as a 'side effect' and while it may be useful to clients, and we allow them space to achieve this, is not central to the approach.

Given this fit it can be considered a 'brief' approach and research into brief therapies can be considered relevant to Solution Focused Therapy.

Freud as the first brief therapist!

All models are beginning to recognize the effectiveness of 'brief' approaches. What surprised us initially was that, 'psychodynamically oriented approaches to brief therapy are most numerous' (Koss and Butcher, 'Research on Brief Psychotherapy' in Garfield and Bergin, 1971, p. 629). Psychoanalytical therapy is still perceived as looking at the past, a long and expensive process, but it can be very brief indeed.

The excellent paper by Alex Coren (Coren, 1996) shows that the history of psychoanalysis is interesting. Freud appears to have been more flexible than his followers in his use of 'brief' therapy. His treatment of Bruno Walter, the conductor, in 1906 is of interest. The eminent conductor had developed an arm ailment which meant he suffered such pain that he could not use his arm for conducting or playing the piano (Walter, 1947, p. 182). He saw Freud and was, '. . . resigned to submit to months of soul searching. The consultation took a course I had not foreseen. Instead of questioning me about sexual aberrations in infancy, as my layman's ignorance had led me to expect, *Freud examined my arm briefly*'. Freud went on to ask Walter if he had ever been to Sicily. He said Walter was to leave immediately, forget about his arm and the opera and do nothing for a few weeks but use his eyes. Walter went to Sicily. His '. . . soul and mind were greatly benefited by the additional knowledge I had gained of Hellenism, but not my arm'.

When Walter returned to Vienna, Freud's advice at the next session was to conduct. Walter describes the following exchange (which sounds strangely familiar to us even ninety one years later).

Walter: 'But I can't move my arm.'
Freud: 'Try it at any rate.'
Walter: 'And what if I should have to stop?'
Freud: 'You won't have to stop.'

Walter: 'Can I take it upon myself the responsibility of possibly upsetting a performance?'
Freud: 'I'll take the responsibility.'

Walter conducted and '. . . there were times when I forgot my arm over
the music. I noticed that at my next session with Freud that he
attached particular importance to my forgetting', and he succeeded in
returning to the conductor's dais within six interviews. Freud using
distraction, myth, a focus on eyes instead of ears (and arm) and amplifying exceptions (forgetting?). Surely not! Actually, no. Psychoanalysts
would see his actions as Freud using techniques to deal with 'resistance, therapeutic passivity and dependence'. However, 'successful'
therapy is perhaps a universal language of its own and it is fitting
that each approach explains technique according to its own body of
knowledge.

In this sense, Freud was the 'original brief therapist' (Alex Coren).
There seems to be an overlap in all good practice. Walter's was not
an isolated case. In 1908 Gustav Mahler's treatment consisted of one
4-hour session. Garcia (1990) felt that, 'Despite (or I suspect because
of) being the founder of psychoanalysis, Freud was far from being an
inflexible despot when it came to its therapeutic application. He happened to believe that psychoanalysis as a therapy was at best first
among equals.'

Freud also treated a 'patient' (as he called them) known as Katharina
in one session during his holiday in the Austrian mountains (Breuer
and Freud, 1944).

Freud's brief cures, like his atypical family ones, are found not in his
works but in biographies about him, since these ideas may not have
fitted neatly with the theory he was struggling to develop.

Davanloo (1978) suggested that psychoanalysis had forgotten
Freud's flexibility when he stated, 'We have lost the art of curing
people briefly'. There is a body of research that is, however, regaining
this art, introducing the idea that therapy can be brief to the psychodynamic field, and which also has implications for Solution Focused
Therapy.

General Brief Therapy research

How brief is brief? Ferenczi (1960) tried to keep analysis short by suggesting the analyst adopt a more active, directive role. Alexander and
French suggested brief therapy be limited to 40 sessions but Koss and
Butcher point out that they often concluded their own cases in three
sessions! In the context of a Kleinian analysis of five years three times

a week, 40 sessions was pretty radical! (Alexander and French, 1946). David Malan reduced this to 20 sessions (Malan, 1992). Coren (1996) states that his student counselling service, 'had gone, because of the overwhelming demand and the length of the waiting list, from routinely offering students a minimum of six sessions, to being unable to guarantee students more than an initial consultation and one follow-up session'. Nationally, he states that the average number of sessions is around four. So from within one field (psychoanalysis) we find variations in approach, a general acceptance that briefer approaches are warranted and great discussion about, 'How brief is brief?'.

Clients appear to want their problems worked on in a focused manner and in a surprisingly low number of sessions. Studies suggest that they vote for brief therapy with their feet! In fact, research indicates that the mean number of sessions of therapy that clients attend is somewhere between 5 and 6! (Garfield, 1971, 1989; Garfield and Kurtz, 1952).

Waltzlawick *et al.*, at the Mental Research Institute, Paolo Alto, set a ten session limit on therapy for their clients but they also found that 72 per cent of their cases were 'successful' (40 per cent complete relief of the presenting complaint and 32 per cent clear and considerable improvement) within an average of seven sessions (Waltzlawick *et al.*, 1974).

Even with the what are viewed as 'difficult' diagnosis such as clients who abuse alcohol, treatment can be effective in a surprisingly short time. Cummings *et al.* sampled 15 000 clients and found treatment lasting an average of six sessions produced a significant impact on the problem drinker (Cummings *et al.*, 1990).

Koss and Butcher found, when looking at the research, that as many brief clinicians recommended one to six sessions as recommended the longer ten to 25 session treatments.

Solution Focused Therapy sets no fixed limit but as we will discuss later, across solution focused literature, the average number of sessions required prior to negotiated termination of therapy is around four. However, Moshe Talmon (1990) has developed a model aimed at a single session therapy (see p. 5).

When less is more. Effectiveness of Brief Therapy

Question: 'Is long term therapy "better" for clients than brief therapy?' Koss and Butcher found that as many clinicians recommended one to six sessions as recommended the longer ten to 25 session treatments.

In terms of effectiveness, Koss and Butcher found that studies comparing brief therapy against long-term therapy have found equal effectiveness. If brief methods are equally effective then it can be argued that they are more cost efficient than long-term psychotherapy (needing less therapist time and less client time) and worth consideration. See also Howard *et al.* (1986) and Smith *et al.* (1980).

Fisher reported that six sessions were as effective as 12 and that they were both as effective as unlimited therapy (Fisher, 1980). He also found that things actually improved over time after brief therapy, suggesting that it is more than a 'sticking plaster' but can actually assist long-term change (Fisher, 1984).

Wallerstein published research in 1986 and 1989 showing that in a 12-year study at the Menninger clinic (a psychoanalytic treatment clinic and training institution) clients who received brief psychoanalytic treatment reported benefits equal to those reported by clients who had undergone 'extensive' long-term psychoanalytic treatment (Wallerstein, 1986, 1989).

Studies into the effectiveness of brief psychotherapy report approximate improvement in 70 per cent of cases. Koss and Butcher cite the following studies: Baxter and Beaulieu (1976, Unpublished Manuscript cited in Koss and Butcher); Sifenos (1972, 1975) and Steward (1972). These studies seem to suggest that Solution Focused Therapy (considered later) is as effective as other brief approaches since it shows an approximate 70 per cent success rate on follow-up. In fact Koss and Butcher suggest, 'Overall there is little support for a statement of significant superiority for any of the diverse approaches to brief psychotherapy examined to date'.

Sloane *et al.* (1975) looked at comparing brief behavioural approaches with brief psychodynamic methods and found no significant differences between the approaches. Sloane suggested that behaviour therapy seemed to produce change slightly sooner and produced more focused change than analytic therapy but differences were not highly significant. This may suggest that the future focus and scaling of Solution Therapy may be slightly more useful than interpretation, but more study is needed. Therefore, brief approaches appear to be as effective as long-term therapy despite a 'common sense' view that longer term work is more effective.

Who is suitable?

General studies into the suitability of certain clients as opposed to others seem to support our idea that we will use solution focused questions to find out what will help a particular client, rather than exclude them because of diagnostic label, social class, history, etc. In effect, we don't know who it will work with until we ask some questions and the clients indicate whether this is what they want from therapy; whether they can put up with us.

Lambert made the point that clinicians seem to, '. . . specify, on the basis of intuition and theoretical bias, the clients that are most suitable for particular brief therapy interventions, without evaluating these assumptions in a formal research design. Thus there has been a failure to test the suitability of these treatments with some patients who are presumed unsuitable, but who may very well profit from the approach' (Lambert, 1979).

Psychodynamic and behavioural brief treatments initially focused on particular clients, suggesting certain criteria were linked to successful outcomes, particularly client motivation (Sifenos, 1975). In Solution Therapy motivation is not a fixed and measurable entity, but varies according to whether the therapist has connected with the client's goal sufficiently for the client to take an interest in proceedings! To consider clients as unsuitable on motivational grounds therefore does not apply.

Sifenos (1975) seconded by Mann (1973) developed a list of selection criteria for brief therapy (psychodynamic) which cited:

1. above average intelligence;
2. at least one meaningful relation with another person during the patient's lifetime;
3. an emotional crisis;
4. ability to interact well with the interviewing psychiatrist and to express feeling;
5. motivation to work hard during psychotherapy;
6. a specific chief complaint.

Budman and Stone (1983) suggested that selection criteria exclude those 'deemed less desirable by clinicians practising in any modality'. They went on to quote studies suggesting that as few as 6 per cent of an inpatient population and 20 per cent of out-patients met Sifenos' (1975) criteria for 'motivation' therapy. Since clients can not be labelled and placed into easy categories and most of our clients do not fall within Sifenos' indicators of motivation for success in therapy (yet still do very well), we feel that excluding clients from a first session on theoretical criteria is unwarranted and we will see anyone for the first session. We see session one as treatment *and* assessment for suitability at the same time.

Koss and Butcher suggest (1971, p. 662): 'It does not appear that acute onset, good previous judgement to life, good ability to relate, a focal problem, high initial motivation, lower socio-economic class, current crisis, or a host of other determining variables related to the patient have been shown to be any more highly related to outcome in brief therapy than in longer term therapies.'

What about the client's role in making Brief Therapy effective?

Research has repeatedly suggested that the client's role in therapy, their relationship with the therapist, their inclusion in the therapy process and their ownership of change is vital to the success of a therapeutic interaction. Far from always being stuck or 'helpless' they have the most important effect on outcome. They also bring changes at home, before even seeing us.

Endicott and Endicott (1963) found that 9 per cent of clients with a diagnosis of 'schizophrenia' and 52 per cent of most other patients spontaneously improve without any treatment!

David Malan (1975) at the Tavistock Clinic, London, followed up 45 'untreated neurotic patients' that were seen for a single session and dropped out or were assessed but found 'not suitable' for psychodynamic treatment. Malan and his colleagues followed these clients' progress between 2 and 9 years after therapy. He found that 51 per cent were improved symptomatically and 24 per cent improved 'psychodynamically'. He felt that single session clients provided, 'not only direct evidence of therapeutic mechanisms in everyday life, but also, quite unexpectedly, evidence about the therapeutic effects of single interviews' (p. 110). He summarized by saying, 'Finally, dynamically oriented psychiatrists should be aware of the powerful potential therapeutic effect both of telling a patient that he must take responsibility for his own life, and of reassuring him that he can manage without therapeutic help.' Frances and Clarkin (1981) summarized 17 well-controlled studies and found an average spontaneous remission rate of 43 per cent.

Solution Therapy utilizes clients' abilities to make change spontaneously and without the therapeutic intervention (known as 'pre-session change') by using exception questions and the positive 'How can we help?' opening which does not assume the client is stuck. This communicates confidence that change is possible (and may have already occurred) and allows them to disclose strengths as well as difficulties. It can be said to be all about maintaining a positive and respectful stance to the client, so maximizing the therapeutic relationship. At a simple level this is done by involving the client at every stage of the therapeutic process (not hypothesizing without them, asking their opinion, using open questions, etc.) and also by allowing them to define the focus of therapeutic conversations, discuss their goals and dreams and credit themselves with their own successes. The miracle, scale, exception and relationship questions all help in this process of seeing the client as the expert in their own difficulty. Research into the importance of the client in Brief Therapy seems to support this attitude. The fact that Solution Therapists ask open questions and invite answers to the Miracle, relationship and exception questions at great length and depth may also fit with research that the more clients say in sessions, the better the outcome.

Gomes-Schwartz (1978) looked at the relationships between patients' and therapists' actions and their effect on the outcome of therapy. She found that patient involvement was the best predictor of outcome. The therapeutic relationship was of utmost importance to the result of the therapy: 'The variables that best predicted change were not related to therapeutic techniques but to the positiveness of the patient's attitude toward the therapist and his commitment to work at changing.'

Marzarli *et al.* (1981) used his earlier work to develop a 'therapeutic alliance scale' based on audiotapes of sessions. They found that if the clients' contribution to this scale was high, if they made a strong positive contribution to the therapeutic alliance and were active in the session, they had good outcomes.

McDaniel *et al.* (1981) looked at the total number of utterances made by clients during sessions and found that those clients who improved more had participated in the sessions more; in layman's terms they had been talking to the therapist more.

Staples and Sloane (1970) found that the more the client talked relative to the therapist, the greater they improved, and also that the longer the client's average 'utterances' were, the greater the improvement: Sloane's later research also supported this (1975).

Budman and Gurman (1983) highlighted the importance of the client's 'real life' outside of therapy as opposed to the behaviour in the consulting room, supporting the practice of giving tasks and homework assignments.

Liberman *et al.* (1974) reinforced the importance of the clients' own involvement in solving their difficulties by showing that clients who achieved changes that resulted from their own efforts to overcome a difficulty maintained their progress longer than clients who believed that changes were due to placebo medication. Giving the client ownership of the eventual solution and credit for the hard work involved in change would therefore seem to have a therapeutic effect (cited in Frank, 1974).

Finally, Frank (1974) reminds us of the importance of the central theme in the effectiveness of brief therapy (and the aim of Solution Therapy): 'The quality of the therapeutic interaction, to which the patient, therapist and therapeutic model contribute, is probably the major determinant of short term therapeutic response.'

What should the therapist do to ensure effectiveness?

It appears that therapists should make use of the client's presenting difficulty as a starting point for therapy and also ensure that a focus is kept during the sessions, that they are purposeful. The focus is what the client presents as the focus or to quote Steve de Shazer, 'What you've got is what you've got'. Working on the presenting difficulty brought by the client rather than another agenda is recognized as an important part of most brief therapy.

Koss and Butcher (1971) state that a client 'frequently brings to therapy an idea of the symptom he or she would most like to alleviate. Most clinicians suggest that the patient have major input in choosing the goals of limited therapy'.

Small (1971) suggests that, 'Achievement and maintenance of a focus can be regardless the single most important technical aspect of brief psychotherapy'.

Budman and Gurman (1983) suggest that the major technical error related to negative outcomes in brief work is the failure of the therapist to structure or focus the sessions. The suggestion by most brief therapists is that this focus is found in the first session. Negotiating this focus is the aim of the first session of Solution Therapy and explains why we ask the Miracle Question early on whenever appropriate.

The therapist can also be enthusiastic, believe in their approach and use its techniques and this may influence outcome. Malan (1976) described his idea that the therapist's enthusiasm has an important effect on therapeutic outcome. He had noticed that many young therapists describe dramatic cures early on in their careers that they are unable to recreate later. The wear and tear on the therapist's enthusiasm for their model, he feels, may be responsible for this.

Lerner and Fiske (1973) reported that the attitude of, 'conviction in counsellors, their belief that they could help, even in difficult circumstances', was very important.

Swensen (1972) confirmed that a counsellor characteristic called 'commitment' was very significant in influencing the outcomes of counselling in a positive direction. Such commitment is shown in Solution Therapy by pre-suppositional questions such as, 'What helps?', and, 'What's better?', and the general attitude of the therapist reinforcing clients' existing solution behaviours and treating 'impossible cases' as the same as any case.

Koss and Butcher (1971) summarize by saying that, 'in addition to being a clearly viable clinical treatment option, brief psychotherapy has been shown to have value as a long-term therapy analogue and as a format for studying, with some precision, the effectiveness of specific intervention techniques on specific problems' (p. 663).

And so

Brief therapies report frequent success of 70 per cent or so. They appear to be as effective as long-term therapies and there is so far no discernible difference in outcome accorded to any particular model. They allow clients who would have been excluded from long-term therapy to be seen, help waiting lists and reduce the usage of medical services. A major factor in their success or failure is whether the client is involved and can build a positive relationship with the therapist and whether the therapist can keep the sessions in focus (a focus that is more successful if it links the past to the present and the present to what the client identifies as the problem). Some brief therapies also make use of the fact that clients change prior to attending for therapy and may have even solved their difficulty before the therapist asks his carefully considered question or makes his fabulous intervention!

Solution Focused Therapy research

William Hudson O'Hanlon and Brian Cade (1993) described the impact of de Shazer's work on the field of brief therapy in their book:

> In our opinion, the work of Steve de Shazer and his colleagues at the Brief Family Therapy Centre in Milwaukee has represented one of the most interesting developments in the field of brief therapy over this last decade. While many seem to have become concerned with building elaborate theoretical castles, often based on the works of various anthropologists, physicists, and biologists, de Shazer and his colleagues have continued to work towards clearer and more precise descriptions and definitions of the essence of effective therapy.

As discussed elsewhere, Solution Focused Therapy is not brief by design. There is no set number of sessions. However, it can be said to meet general criteria for 'good practice' suggested by the research quoted above. It meets these areas of good practice by:

1. its techniques which ensure a focus to sessions (vital to achieving effective therapy in a short space of time);

2. its ability to accept a client's initial definition of a difficulty (vital in involving them in therapy, encouraging cooperation and ensuring clients are motivated to contribute to the session, thus maximizing the likelihood of success);
3. its future orientation and use of homework tasks that clients can relate to their own solutions (and so 'own change' for themselves, rather than attribute such change to the therapist).

These fit with the research into effective short-term therapy (including the definitions of good brief therapy provided by practitioners of *other* models, discussed above). Beyebach *et al.* (1996) undertook research on the process of Solution-Focused Brief Therapy. They discovered that of 39 out patients in mental health 80% achieved their goal with an average of 5 sessions and a mean of 33 minutes per session. Therapy was more effective if there were concrete goals established and an indication of pre-session change given by the client.

Brief (by outcome) but with enduring change: The Milwaukee Team Studies

de Shazer *et al.* (1986) at the Brief Family Therapy Centre in Milwaukee, USA, found that their 'average number of sessions per client has declined from 6 sessions for 1600 cases (1978 through 1983) to fewer than 5 sessions for 500 cases in 1984'. By 1993 Hopwood was able to state that, at the Brief Family Therapy Centre, 'For the past five years we have averaged 4.5 sessions per case and 97% of the cases come for fewer than 10 sessions. We have no selection criteria and we see anyone who comes to see us' (Hopwood, 1992, Introductory Lecture at the *Advanced Residency Training BFTC*, Milwaukee, USA). The Milwaukee team also conducted a follow-up study in 1986. Between 1978 and 1983 they had seen 1000 cases. They followed up 25 per cent (250) of this number using an independent person who had no contact with the case to make telephone contact: '. . . 72% either met their goal for therapy or felt that significant improvement had been made so that further therapy was not necessary.' This, de Shazer states, is similar to the success rate reported by time limited brief therapists such as Weakland, who found 'a similar rate within an average of 7 sessions' (de Shazer *et al.*, 1986).

De Shazer *et al.* (1986) also conducted another small follow-up study at six months to one year after discharge from the Brief Therapy Centre. His team were only able to contact 28 of the 56 clients in the original 'formula first session task' project (they were looking at sessions where a formula 'Notice what is happening that you would like to keep happening for next time' intervention question was asked). Of these clients, when asked, 'when you came to therapy, your main complaint was. . . . Is that better, the same, worse?'. Twenty-three of the 28 reported that their complaint was better. The average number of sessions per case was five. The Milwaukee team suggested in the same paper that, 'Rapid changes can be enduring', that long-lasting change can be evident from only a few sessions and, in fact, that the skills clients use to solve their difficulties through Solution Focused Therapy can go on to help them resolve further problems without recourse to therapy. De Shazer *et al.* state: 'When asked: During therapy, you noticed a change in (something our records indicated they reported during the second session), is this continuing?', 23 of the 28 responded in the affirmative.' When the clients were asked about further improvements, 'Have any old problems that were not directly dealt with in therapy improved since you finished at Brief Family Therapy Centre?', the Milwaukee team found that 15 of the 28 'reported improvements in areas not dealt with at all in therapy'. So do clients go on getting better even after only a few sessions of therapy?

Iseabeart and de Shazer (1997) have submitted a paper on an alcohol programme run at St Johns Hospital in Brugge. Clients spend a maximum of three weeks as inpatients and then receive out patient follow-up. In a 250 case telephone review at 5 years after treatment 49.1 per cent were abstinent, 25 per cent practiced controlled drinking of whom 58 per cent had no problems. Eighty-eight per cent 'felt good'; 79 per cent had had no further treatment during that time and 75 per cent had not had a relapse into alcohol abuse (uncommon in alcohol follow-ups).

This area of interest was again studied by Kiser and Nunnally at the Brief Family Therapy Centre. They used the same questions as those used by Watzlawick *et al.* at the Mental Research Institute (1974) and found an 80.4 per cent success rate (65.6 per cent of the clients met their goal and 14.7 per cent made 'significant improvement') within an average of 4.6 sessions. When re-contacted at 18 months, the success rate had *increased* to 86 per cent. Sixty-seven per cent of the clients reported improvements in other areas since the end of therapy (Kiser, 1988). This suggests that solution focused 'skills' can continue to be applied by clients to new problems that occur later in their lives. We feel that the therapy orients the client to a new way of finding solutions and could be considered 'psycho-educational'. Clients can then apply solution focused thinking to future problems as they occur, rather than having to return to therapy to sort things out.

De Jong and Hopwood (1996) conducted outcome research at the Brief Therapy Centre between 1992 and 1993. Two hundred and seventy-five clients broke down in 93 per cent clients under 45 years of age. Forty-five per cent reported their goal was achieved, 32 per cent reported some progress. In Berg and Dejong (1996) 275 cases were asked a scaling question pre- and immediately post therapy, 25 per cent reported significant progress; 49 per cent moderate progress; 26 per cent no progress.

Weiner Davies *et al*. (1987) looked at utilizing changes made by clients prior to therapy and she found change had often already begun without us!: 'Many times people notice in between the time they make the appointment for therapy and the first session that things already seem different'. This fits with evidence of client's changing before seeing a therapist. Noonan (1973) followed-up clients who asked for an appointment but never attended. Thirty-five per cent put their non-attendance down to improvement between the time they called and the first appointment.

Diane Iveson (1992), followed de Shazer's follow-up methodology in researching a London Brief Solution Focused Clinic. Her results yielded comparable success rates with de Shazer within a comparably few number of sessions. Eakes *et al*. conducted a pilot study on 'Family Centred' brief solution focused therapy with Schizophrenia, using experimental and control groups (of five families each only). Using a Family Environment Scale, clients in the experimental group showed a significant increase in expressiveness, active recreational orientation and a decrease in levels of incongruence. Interestingly, they opted for a reflecting team but not to use the miracle question. Macdonald (1994) found that at a one year follow-up of 41 adult psychiatric cases 70 per cent improved. There was an equal outome for all social classes with an average of 3.71 sessions needed. Long standing problems did less well.

Research in Scotland: The work of the Angus Team

Gerry Brophy and Kenny Gouck (1995) of Angus NHS Trust researched their use of Solution Focused Therapy following training from the authors in the model (1993). They adapted the model for use in a community psychiatric nursing service in Angus. They audited their service to gain an estimate of the clinical and cost effectiveness of Solution Focused work. They audited a representative sample of clients who received Solution Therapy in Angus between 1st April 1994 and 31st March 1995 (53 clients).

Reasons for referral included depression, anxiety, obsessive compulsive disorder, bereavement, survivors of sexual abuse, eating disorders, post-natal depression, agoraphobia, relationship problems, multiple sclerosis, bereavement and post-traumatic stress disorder. Sixty per cent of the clients were referred for help with anxiety or depression. Only one client (2 per cent) attended for ten sessions with 77 per cent attending for one to four sessions and 21 per cent for five to eight sessions.

They divided discharges into two groups, self discharges (64 per cent) and those discharged through not attending their last session (36 per cent). Of the group that did not attend their last session, 74 per cent had rated themselves as an 8 to 10 on their 'Where are you now' scale. Four per cent (two clients) re-referred themselves within a year but they both presented with different problems from their initial referral. Interestingly, they requested Solution Focused Therapy as their treatment of choice.

Brophy and Gouck went on to state that 'S.F.T. is both clinically and cost effective'.

Single session therapy: Moshe Talmon's work

Treatment is often much briefer than we would expect. To a large extent, the long history, innovative nature and wide acceptance of analytic ideas in our culture and our professional training encourage us (and the public) to consider anything of benefit to be of long duration. This 'therapeutic myth' has coloured our view of our work. Therapists have many 'single sessions' with clients and these have been considered as 'flukes'. Therapists have even been trained to see clients

leaving therapy after only a few sessions as a sign of their illness rather than health. For instance, psychoanalysts saw this as a 'flight into health' with the client escaping, rather than facing the painful but necessary period of working on their difficulties. Therapists often feel that clients were not ready for therapy or that they could not cope with it, that they themselves have failed to engage the client or have failed in some other way and the whole area of one and two session episodes took on an air of hopelessness.

Silverman and Beech (1979) studied 'drop outs' in a community mental health centre and saw things differently. They felt that the idea drop outs represented a failure by the client or therapist was 'clearly untenable'. They interviewed clients considered to be 'drop outs' and found that almost 80 per cent reported that their problems had been solved and 70 per cent reported satisfaction with the service they received.

While more negative rationales for single sessions *may* in some cases be so, Moshe Talmon researched the phenomenon of single sessions and put them in a different light in his book, *Single Session Therapy* (Talmon, 1990).

While working for a department of psychiatry in California he entered the department chief's office to discuss a case. He saw some computer printouts on the desk which the chief had ordered eight years previously and read only occasionally. They were titled, 'Number of visits per patient; Reporting period for prior 12 months'. Moshe Talmon asked for them out of interest and was 'astonished' by what he found contained in the data. The most frequent length of therapy for every therapist in the department was one session. Thirty per cent of all clients chose to come for only one session in a one-year period. Even when no fee was involved and further sessions offered they chose not to keep their second appointment but also chose not to go elsewhere for therapy! The therapist's personal model had no impact on the percentage of single sessions in their total practice. Talmon found that a psychologist trained in traditional psychoanalysis saw 48 per cent of his clients for one session, a social worker trained in object relations theory saw 55 per cent for a single session and a psychiatrist, believing in a biological model of mental illness, saw 50 per cent once in a one-year period.

Looking at the literature about single sessions in therapy, Moshe Talmon found that this high number of single sessions had been well-documented elsewhere, for example:

1. Kogan (1957) found that out of 250 new cases seen in one month at the Family Services Division in New York, 141 (56 per cent) were closed after one interview.
2. Spoerl (1975) found 36 per cent of 6708 clients seen in 1972 at a private clinic made only one visit despite the fact that their insurance covered them for the first ten visits.
3. Bloom (1975) studied public and private mental health systems in Colorado for two years between 1969 and 1971 and found that of 1,572 first admission out-patients 32 per cent were seen for a single session of therapy.
4. Morano (1989) in a letter to Moshe Talmon stated community health services in Prince William County, Virginia see 80 per cent of patients for a single session.

Intrigued by this, Talmon contacted all 200 of the clients he had seen for a single session. He also had a number of them contacted at random by a neutral postdoctoral student, who had no contact with the cases, to reduce any 'demand characteristics' caused by clients responding to the therapist that saw them. Seventy-eight per cent said they had got what they wanted from the therapy in one session. Those that had experienced no change gave 'reality explanations' such as, 'not being able to take time off work' and only 10 per cent did not like the therapist or the outcome of the session. This correlates with Kogan's

1957 study which found that in single session cases at follow-up interviews a substantial proportion reported reality-based factors which
prevented the continuation of improvement.

Moshe Talmon goes on in his book to describe a pre-planned structure to sessions aiming at single session therapy. He focuses on exception finding, building on clients' strengths and abilities, cooperating
with their frame, uses compliments and homework tasks and also 'pre-
session change' questions. Talmon uses a very eclectic mix to achieve
his results, using pre-session contacts to begin the process of change.
While not exclusively 'solution focused', his book is well worth reading
and his approach is fascinating. He empowers his clients, trying for
a fit between tasks and the client's beliefs, preferring cooperation.
He explains, 'Alexander Levine, an oncologist from the University of
California, Los Angeles, found that 60 per cent of cancer patients
treated on an out-patient basis who were prescribed chemotherapy
medications later had no trace of medication in their blood samples
(Siegel, 1986). If therapists want to prescribe, for example, anti-
depressants, they should find out first whether the patient believes in
using pills' (Talmon, 1990, p. 69).

Our own findings

Being a busy psychiatric team we took the opportunity, prior to training in Milwaukee and after our return, to look at the statistical returns
of our two separate Solution Focused clinics within the Trust for
which we work. Both had different settings, culturally one existed
autonomously as part of a day hospital and the other existed rather
unusually as an out-patient service in a psychodynamically-oriented
unit. The clinics had different staff teams. The returns on attendance,
turn-up rates and average number of sessions were interesting since
they corresponded with de Shazer's research. The sample groups were
of 60 clients at the day-hospital clinic and 75 clients in 1991 and 61
clients in 1992 at the other clinic.

In 1991 we studied one year of using the model in our day-hospital
clinic. One hundred and ninety-four sessions were available to clients
and an 83.5 per cent turn-up rate was recorded with only nine clients
out of 32 cancelling without contacting the clinic (higher than in the
previous five years!; not attending for a second session was much more
common with other models, suggesting clients did not feel engaged by
the first session).

We found that our average number of sessions, seeing any diagnosis
as part of our psychiatric out-patient clinics at the day hospital, fell
from 11.5 using a systemic model of therapy to 3.05 using Solution

Focused Therapy. The range was one to nine sessions with all discharges being mutually agreed when the client felt they had met their initial goals. No one was 'fired' (see Hawkes and Wilgosh, 1991).

In a separate clinic run in a therapeutic community out-patients department, two of the authors found a turn-up rate of 85 per cent for second sessions or beyond (which had increased from 56 per cent the previous year using a systemic model). The average number of sessions was 3.8, duplicating the day-hospital figures in a totally different unit and context (Hawkes and Marsh, 1991). Such a low average number of sessions appear frequently in Solution Therapy research, for instance, Johnson and Lambert (1997) compared 27 cases of theirs with controlled outcome data with 198 cases at a university public mental health centre. Both methods suggested that 45 per cent of clients were considered to be recovered using objective criteria (OQ–45). Solution Focused Therapy clients did so in an average of three sessions while the centre's clients took 26!

In 1992 Hawkes found referrals for this clinic had increased by 90 per cent following the outcomes of the 1991 sessions and a 30 per cent increase in GP referrals was evident as they began to see the benefits of referring clients to Solution Focused Therapy. The attendance rate was again high at 84 per cent. Sixty-one new referrals were researched and the team found that the average number of sessions was 3.1 with a range of one to eight sessions. Of these, in 81 per cent of cases, the team using a rating scale felt that the clients' goals set in the first session had been met (Hawkes, 1992).

Our initial anxiety was that with such a cooperative approach, dependency would develop in the client. We discussed this issue with de Shazer who sees 'dependent clients' who stay in therapy longer as 'over achievers'. We are now considering a follow-up to de Shazer's paper, 'The Death of Resistance' (de Shazer, 1984) entitled 'The Death of Dependency', since very few clients use the opportunity to return and none in the studies quoted above were re-referred 12 months after discharge. In fact, although all clients at a negotiated last session were offered the chance to re-contact the clinics at a later date should they experience any difficulties, none did. When offered the opportunity to ring their therapist at work in between sessions (bearing in mind some negotiated 'gaps' are as long as six weeks) if difficulties arose, in the course of a whole year of the clinic at the psychotherapy unit, none did.

We instigated a one-year follow-up (1995–6) survey on our recent clients by written questionnaire and are awaiting the data analysis at this time. However, the 'dependency' (in our opinion) never materialized. In fact, the average number of sessions fell to 3.1 from 3.8 as a result of our applying the model more rigorously and adapting it to our client group following our 1992 residency training in Milwaukee. So, using techniques such as compliments and the genuineness of the therapist rigorously, far from creating a dependency in clients, meant they required less therapy.

Conclusions

More research in the field is needed, particularly empirical studies comparing Solution Therapy with behavioural or psychodynamic techniques of brief therapy. However, the model appears as effective as any other brief approach. It meets criteria for good therapy through focus, fit, empowerment and clinical outcome. If a practitioner is interested in empowerment, cost effectiveness and brevity, Solution Therapy becomes an attractive choice. The research in the field of generic brief therapy from practitioners promoting other models validates Solution Therapy's techniques while its own small studies validate its cost effectiveness. It helps its success if the therapist is committed to the model and enthusiastic about it. We have found this, too, to be easy given the model's impact on clients and the clients' impact on the approach.

Exercise

Consider the lay person's view of psychotherapy and counselling. How would the research support or question this view? Should therapy be brief? How would the reader use the research to support their existing practice?

16

What to read:
Useful books about the subject

People say that life is the thing, but I prefer reading.
Logan Pearshall Smith (1931)

As discussed earlier, it is in the practical application of these ideas that the reader can develop the model further and it is in the client's reactions to these questions that practitioners will find the most useful comments on Solution Focused Therapy. Listen to your clients.

One of the most frequent questions at our workshop is, 'What would you recommend to a beginner/expert/intermediate solution focused practitioner?'. Our initial answer, 'All of them', did not cooperate with the person's need to live a real life and 'do therapy' in between reading about doing therapy. With limited time and finance hard decisions have to be made. These are, of course, personal but we will try to give you our version of reality and our suggestions about when to read what. This is not a prescription! We would like you to go out and experiment to find what works for you since you know yourself best!

However, there is now an excellent range of texts on the approach in the form of books from America and Finland and papers from Europe. Related topics such as philosophy, constructivism, the narrative approaches to therapy (Australia and New Zealand) and brief therapies in general provide background knowledge and allow the therapist flexibility.

There follows a non-exhaustive list of literature for consideration by budding Solution Therapists with short comments on the content of each book. Each of the books are as excellent as each other, but those we would consider of interest to the beginner are indicated with a grade from 1 to 3 which indicate those we would suggest readers new to the approach consider first (but it's only our idea on the matter!).

(1) This book is considered essential reading and suitable for beginners with time enough to read only a few texts.
(2) This book is intermediate in that it brings in essential new material and is suitable for beginners but also more advanced practitioners.
(3) This book is vital in our opinion for a rounded view of the approach but may best be appreciated after considering other texts.

Know your allies. Books and notes on their authors

Steve de Shazer has published four books on the approach, three we would consider essential reading at some time in a solution focused career. All of the following are published by W. W. Norton, New York. He uses frequent case material to link theory to text.

Keys to Solutions in Brief Therapy (1985) introduces the approach and considers 'skeleton keys' that can unlock multiple diagnosis. The first book on the approach proper, it is well worth considering to gain an insight into its development and the use of first session formula tasks. (3)

Clues (1985) looks at how solutions develop and how to focus on solutions rather than problems. De Shazer introduced a computer programme 'briefer' to analyse solutions and provide a flow chart for sessions. This idea was of its time and he now rarely discusses the programme, which he found somewhat limited. (3)

Putting Difference to Work (1991) is an excellent exploration of language and how it can be used carefully to enable solutions to develop rather than used to entrap clients in their difficulties by reinforcing problems, diagnosis and the 'seriousness' of the problem. Of interest to practitioners who want to consider the model in more depth alongside the work of philosophers such as Derrida and Wittgenstein but still very readable. (2)

Words Were Originally Magic (1994) is his latest book continuing the progression away from 'how to do therapy' books to more accessible and interesting ideas about therapy itself. Plenty of case examples, easy to read and also profound. Again, probably an intermediate book but beginners could do worse than starting here. (2)

William Hudson O'Hanlon and Michelle Weiner Davies: William Hudson O'Hanlon has published on Solution Focused Brief Therapy, Ericksonian Hypnotherapy and brief approaches in general. He trains in this country regularly and is a very entertaining presenter. Michelle Weiner Davies has published on the approach and its use in divorce cases (*Divorce Busting*, 1992). She appeared on the Oprah Winfrey show with some of her clients.

In Search of Solutions. A New Direction in Psychotherapy (1989): although 8 years old, the lack of jargon and humour in this book as well as the clear attempt to link theory and practice through good case material makes this a good book for beginners to approach. (1)
A Brief Guide to Brief Therapy (1993) is an overview of brief therapy, collecting research and techniques from Solution Therapy, MRI brief therapy and Erickson as well as other fields. Puts brief therapy in context and passes on a wealth of useful information succinctly and entertainingly. (2)

Insoo Kim Berg and Scott D. Miller: Insoo Kim Berg has been credited by de Shazer as actually developing the approach. She is the Director of the Brief Family Therapy Centre in Milwaukee and trains in Britain and Europe frequently. The authors hold her in the highest regard both as a writer and as a practitioner who seems able to develop solutions with clients after a vast amount of 'problem talk' has gone on during a session. Scott D. Miller worked as the Director of Drug and Alcohol Treatment and Training Services with the Milwaukee team until 1993 when he continued in independent practice in Chicago as part of 'Problems to Solutions Inc.'. He trains in Britain and is an accessible and humorous teacher. The authors hope to bring Scott to London to present on alcohol shortly. The following books are also published by W.W. Norton, New York.

Working With the Problem Drinker (1992): although focusing on a particular client group this book is a comprehensive overview of Brief Solution Focused Therapy, illustrating the structure of the sessions, challenging myths about the client group and taking the reader in a step-by-step fashion through the approach. Of interest to every beginner who wants more on how to do Solution Therapy. (1)
The Miracle Method: A Radically New Approach to Problem Drinking (1995) is more than just a reprint of the previous volume as this book is simultaneously a very easy to read distillation of the earlier work, a self-help book and a 'how to do' reference book for Solution Therapists. It makes full use of mnemonics and stimulating questions for the reader and is jargon free. (1)

Yevonne M. Dolan has published and trains in Ericksonian Hypnosis as well as her own unique blending of Solution Focused and Brief Therapy ideas. She specializes in working with adult survivors and presents in London, on topics such as resolving sexual abuse and working with impossible clients. Her publisher is W. W. Norton, New York.

Resolving Sexual Abuse: Solution-Focused Therapy and Ericksonian Hypnosis for Adult Survivors (1991) is a book that re-introduces feelings, emotion and history to the Solution Focused field. Yevonne Dolan uses relaxation/self-hypnosis and practical exercises in her therapy and leaves her clients and readers with an inherent feeling of hope. Essential reading for any practitioner who works with this client group. We argued over the classification of this one since it is so thorough it is suitable for a beginner but is a specialist text. (2).

Ben Furman and Tapani Ahola are Finnish therapists with a humorous and eclectic style. Ben presents in Britain quite frequently and manages to be engaging, persuasive and provocative in equal measure. Their blending of Solution-Focused Brief Therapy, Ericksonian approaches, the work of Michael White and David Epston (narrative theory) and even the provocative work of Frank Farrelly produces a respectful and individualistic hybrid that manages to remain uniquely 'theirs'. In discussion with one of the authors at a workshop in 1991, Ben said, 'You know what I am essentially interested in is *pathology* in great detail (this surprised him). I want to know everything about the *pathology* of health!'. (Author's italics.)

Solution Talk: Hosting Therapeutic Conversations (1992) is a stimulating and humorous book that uses solution focused ideas alongside other approaches. The focus is on respect for people's strengths and ensuring the clients are authors of their own diagnosis, therapy and solutions. Numerous case studies illustrate tough cases that mental health professionals will relate to from their own practice. (2)

Moshe Talmon is frequently cited in our research chapter; he is an expert in single session therapy. His research in the field and thorough structure to maximize the effect of one client/therapist meeting is fascinating. He does not use Solution Focused Therapy in any 'pure sense' but his British presentations are thought-provoking and packed with new ideas about what works with clients.

Single Session Therapy: Maximising the Effect of the First (and often only) Therapeutic Encounter (1990) is a worthwhile read for practitioners looking to expand their ideas and enrich their therapy.

Surprising research and in-depth literature search; also for those 'squeezed' into being as brief as possible by employers/funding, etc. (3)

Jay Haley's Books on Milton Erickson: Jay Haley, the practitioner who (with Chloe Medanes) developed Strategic Family Therapy is also the biographer of Milton Erickson, a task he appears to relish. Erickson's ideas have stimulated hypnotherapists, brief therapists, Family Therapists and psychotherapists from all approaches. His ideas are frequently cited by de Shazer as starting points for the early Brief Solution Focused.

Uncommon Therapy: The Psychiatric Techniques of Milton H. Erickson MD (1973) is one of the Norton's best selling therapy books and the only one on this list so far published at a very reasonable price in paperback! Case studies that are so innovative, thought provoking and humorous that they have been used as teaching tales by therapists ever since. This book does not read like a textbook. It should not be the only book read by a new therapist to the field of Solution Focused work (since it is about Ericksonian Therapy rather than Brief Solution Focused Therapy and since the reader could not necessarily practice clinically any of the techniques described in this publication) but it is an important and accessible text. (1)

Paul Watzlawick and the Mental Research Institute Team: Watzlawick has authored texts on Brief Problem Focused Therapy and co-constructivism. He has interest in 'reality' and 'How do we know what we think we know?'. He uses metaphor and story both clinically and in his writing and he is a pleasure to read, even when addressing complex ideas.

Change: Principles of Problem Formation and Problem Resolution (1974) summarizes the Brief Problem Focused Model developed by the authors at Palo Alto, California. It looks at how common sense attempts to solve a difficulty sometimes make things worse and the use of paradoxes (among other techniques) to resolve problems. (3)
The Situation is Hopeless, But Not Serious: The Pursuit of Unhappiness (1983) is a textbook that makes you relate to your own ways of thinking about difficulties. The whole book is a hilarious and yet true paradoxical intervention, aimed at helping us to make our own lives a misery: 'For those not talented enough to create their own hell, this book offers help and encouragement' (from blurb). Of course, by allowing us to see mechanisms by which we develop unhelpful thinking, the book also suggests we do something different. Good fun. (2)

The Invented Reality: How Do We Know What We Believe We Know? (1984) (Watzlawick is the editor) contains essays on how reality is constructed in the conversations between the client and therapist and therefore how they can co-construct new realities and solve apparently impossible problems. Interesting to further consider the implication of language on reality. (3)

Michael White and David Epston work in Australia and New Zealand and have developed 'Narrative Therapy'. This encourages clients to construct a new view of the world by externalizing the problem, discussing it as if it were a real entity outside the client and nothing to do with them. At times a new diagnostic label is created by the client for the problem. This reduces blame and then allows a collaboration to develop between the therapist and client in order to defeat this very real pain in the behind difficulty! De Shazer sees this work as interesting but different from solution finding therapies since it still focuses on a 'problem', albeit one outside the client. It has led to strong political action and empowerment of user groups, who exchange ways of fighting their difficulties and can band together to do so, such as the 'Anti-Anorexia League' which has formed an action group in more than one continent. Always respectful to clients, even giving them authorship of solutions that are later shared at workshops, e.g., 'This is Bill's solution to this problem', the credit for change stays firmly with the client. It is excellent for use with children. White and Epston have both presented in London and Liverpool respectively.

Narrative Means to Therapeutic Ends (1990) is a collection of their cases and work using their model of Narrative Therapy. (3)

Harvey Ratner, Chris Iveson and Evan George are the first British trainers in Brief Solution Focused Therapy, and they work together as part of the Brief Therapy Practice in London. As a team they frequently host workshops from most of the authors named in this book list. Strongly in the Brief Therapy tradition, this is the only other British publication at present.

Problem to Solution (1990), a paperback which covers the early techniques of the approach with case material and discussion of the stages of therapy as they stood prior to 'working with the problem drinker' in 1992. (1)

We will leave this limited set of suggested literature here. The reader's attention is drawn to the philosophy of Derrida (1978), e.g., *Writing and Difference*, University of Chicago Press, and the later works of Wittgenstein, e.g., *Philosophical Investigations* (1958), Macmillan through their original texts or through biographies of them (which are easier to absorb) but they are **definitely** a (3)! Philosophy is adequately covered in the de Shazer books mentioned earlier. Remember libraries! All of the above bar two are only available as hardbacks.

The Possession of a book becomes a substitute for reading it.
Anthony Burgess (1966)

17

Where to next?: Resources for further information and training

---

When we began reading papers on the approach there was no British training or peer support. Now, thanks to the growth of the approach throughout Europe, it is a different story, with several important resources for practitioners to seek out. It is important to gain training in the approach and peer support through networking and through attending international workshops from authors on the model whenever possible. Luckily, most solution focused trainers write books without jargon and present new ideas in an engaging manner. This makes keeping current a pleasure rather than a chore.

Keeping current through a regular newsletter

Readers are encouraged to subscribe directly to *News of the Difference: A bulletin board for people who do therapy that makes a difference*. It is edited by Dvorah Simon in New York. The cost is minimal but the content and ideas help keep you up to date with current innovations in America and it is great value. Send subscriptions or write to: Dvorah Simon, *News of the Difference*, 392 Central Park West, Apartment 20 U, New York, NY 10025, USA.

Trainers in Solution Focused Therapy

The Authors present workshops on the approach throughout the UK and Europe at introductory and advanced levels. They provide supervision and support in the use of the model. They can be contacted via two addresses and enjoy responding to correspondence, helping to link professionals and talking for hours about Solution related subjects.

Dave Hawkes, 'Solutions in Training', Solution focused training at all levels. 8 Bate Dudley Drive, Bradwell on Sea, Essex CM0 7QG, UK.
Ian Marsh, Solution Therapy Consultants, 175a High Street, Brentwood, Essex, CM14 4SD, UK.
Ron Wilgosh, 4 Barrington Court, Hutton, Brentwood, Essex CM13 1AX, UK.
The Milwaukee Team in America can provide video training tapes, books and their residency training in Brief Solution Focused Therapy. They are the model's originators but are still very accessible and supportive (this book is a result of their advice and support). Contact them at their US address: The Brief Family Therapy Centre, PO Box 13736, Milwaukee, Wisconsin, USA. E-mail: briefftc@aol.com.
The Brief Therapy Practice in London run frequent international workshops, bringing de Shazer, Insoo Kim Berg, Scott Miller, Bill O'Hanlon, Yevonne Dolan, Ben Furman and Moshe Talmon over for training events. Contact them via 4D Shirland Mews, London W9 3DY.
Harry Norman provides solutions focused training, course design, team facilitation and non-managerial supervision. He provides counselling courses for and has links with Bristol University and can be contacted via: 29 Wesley Place, Clifton, Bristol BS8 4YD. You can also e-mail him at 106300.140@compuserve.com.
In Scotland **Gerry Brophy and Kenny Gouck** provide support, networking and training in Solution Focused Therapy. Contact them through, CPN Services, Angus NHS Trust, c/o Abbey Health Centre, Montrose, Angus DD11 1EN.
In the Orkney Islands, **Ewen Taylor** provides a contact point for practitioners interested in keeping current with the solution focused approach. He can be contacted through The Health Centre, New Scapa Road, Kirkwall, Orkney KW15 1BX.
Dr A. J. Macdonald in Cumbria provides an accredited course in 'Solution Focused Brief Therapy' at level 2 with 15 cats points. Contact him via Garlands Hospital, Carlisle, Cumbria CA1 3SX.

The European connection: the European Brief Therapy Association

The European Brief Therapy Association is growing from strength to strength. Set up to network professionals in brief therapy in Europe, Solution Focused Therapists represent a major component of its membership throughout the UK, Ireland, Belgium, France, Germany, Austria, Norway, Finland, Sweden, Spain, Italy, Poland, Bulgaria and the Czech Republic. It runs fascinating conferences that rotate venue throughout its member countries. Presentations are always of the highest standard; Insoo Kim Berg and Steve de Shazer often attend. Workshops are translated into four languages and it is great to be able to debate and discuss the model with other practitioners who understand your viewpoint and have a common ground. The beer is usually good too! For further information on membership contact: EBTA, 16 Rue de Pali Kao 75020, Paris, France. E-mail: homepage:http://hem 1. Passagen.se/solution/eb ta.htm.

Other web sites include:

- EBTA Newsletter website: http://home1.swipnet.se/~w-11664/ EBTANews.html
- SFTWebpage:http://rdz.stjohns.edu/sft/
- Briefftc:http://www/brief-therapy.org
- Sft forum:listserv@maelstrom.stjohns.edu

It is important to scan the professional magazines for articles and also to publish case studies, research, statistical audits and specialist applications of the model. It is still growing and developing and too much successful work does not find its way into print so *make a contribution* to the development of Solution Focused Therapy as we focus on its future in the next millennium.

Bibliography

Alexander, F. and French, T. M. (1946). *Psychoanalytic Therapy: Principles and Applications*. Ronald Press.

Alvarez, A. (1974). *The Savage God: A Study of Suicide*. Penguin Books.

Anderson, H. and Golishian, H. A. (1989). Dialogic rather than interventionist: an interview by L. Winderman. *Family Therapy News* **Nov/Dec**, 11.

Bateson, G. (1972). *Steps to an Ecology of Mind*. Ballantine Books.

Berg, I. K. and Dejong, P. (1996). Solution building conversations: coconstructing a sense of competence with clients. *Families in Society*, **77** (6), 376–391.

Berg, I. K. and Miller, S. D. (1992). *Working With The Problem Drinker*. W. W. Norton.

Berg, I. K. and Miller, S. D. (1995). *The Miracle Method: A Radically New Approach to Problem Drinking*. W. W. Norton.

Beyebach, M., Morejon, A. R., Palenzuela, D. L., Rodriguez-Arias, J. L. (1996). Cited in S. D. Miller, M. A. Hubble and B. L. Duncan (eds) *Handbook of Solution Focused Brief Therapy*. Jossey Bass, pp. 299–334.

Bion, W. R. (ed.) (1980). *Bion in New York and Sao Paulo*. Perthshire Clunie Press.

Bloom, B. L. (1975). *Changing Patterns of Psychiatric Care*. Human Sciences Press.

Bradshaw, T. and Haddock, G. (1995). Psychological management of schizophrenia symptoms. *Mental Health Nursing*, **15** (1), 21–23.

Breuer, R. J. and Freud, S. (1944). Studies in Hysteria. In J. Strachey (ed.) *The Complete Psychological Works of Sigmund Freud Vol 2.* Hogarth Press (originally published in 1893).

Brooking, J. and Minghella, E. (1987). Parasuicide. *Nursing Times*, **83** (21), 40–44.

Brophy, G. and Gouck, K. (1995). Solution Focused Brief Therapy, the Work Of The Solution Focused Clinic in Angus. Unpublished paper for Angus NHS Trust.

Budman, S. H. and Gurman, A. (1983). The practice of brief therapy. *Professional Psychology: Research and Practice*, **14**, 277–292.

Budman, S. H. and Stone, J. (1983). Advances in brief psychotherapy: A review of recent literature. *Hospital and Community Psychiatry*, **34**, 939–946.

Burgess, A. (1966). *New York Times Book Review* 4 December, p. 74.

Coren, A. (1996). Brief Therapy base metal or pure gold? *Psychodynamic Counselling*, 2.1 (Feb), 22–38.

Cummings, N. A. and Follette, W. T. (1976). Brief Psychotherapy and Medical Utilization. In H. Dorken (ed.) *The Psychologist Today: New Developments in Law, Health Insurance and Health Practice.* Jossey Bass, pp. 165–174.

Davanloo (1978). *Basic Principles and Techniques in Short Term Dynamic Psychotherapy.* S.P. Medical and Scientific Books.

Dejong, P. and Hopwood, L. E. (1996). Cited in S. D. Miller, M. A. Hubble and B. L. Duncan (eds) *Handbook of Solution Focused Brief Therapy.* Jossey Bass, pp. 272–298.

Derrida, J. (1978). *Writing and Difference.* University of Chicago Press.

de Shazer, S. (1984). The death resistance. *Family Process*, 23, 11–17.

de Shazer, S. (1985). *Clues: Investigating Solutions in Brief Therapy.* W. W. Norton.

de Shazer, S. (1988). *Key Solutions in Brief Therapy.* W. W. Norton.

de Shazer, S. (1991). *Putting Difference to Work.* W. W. Norton.

de Shazer, S. (1994). *Words Were Originally Magic.* W. W. Norton.

de Shazer, S., Berg, I. K., Lipchik, E., Nunnally, E., Gingerich, W. and Weiner Davis, M. (1987). Brief Therapy Focused Solution Development. *Family Process*, **25**, 207–221.

Dolan, Y. M. (1991). *Resolving Sexual Abuse: Solution-Focused Therapy and Ericksonian Hypnosis for Adult Survivors.* W. W. Norton.

Eakes, G., Walsh, S., Markowski, M., Cain, H. and Swanson, M. (1997). Family Centred Brief Solution Focused Therapy with chronic schizophrenia: a pilot study. *Journal of Family Therapy*, **19**, 145–158.

Endicott, N. A. and Endicott, J. (1963). Improvements in untreated psychiatric patients. *Archives of General Psychiatry*, **9**, 575–585.

Ferenczi, S. (1960). The further development of an active therapy in psychoanalysis. In J. Richman (ed.) *Further Contributions in the Theory and Techniques of Psychoanalysis*. Hogarth, pp. 198–216.

Fisher, S. (1980). The use of time limits in Brief Psychotherapy, a comparison of six session, twelve session and unlimited treatment of families. *Family Process*, **19**, 377–392.

Fisher, S. (1984). Time Limited Brief Therapy with families: A One Year Follow Up Study. *Family Process*, **23**, 101–106.

Frances, A. and Clarkin, J. F. (1981). No treatment as the prescription of choice. *Archives of General Psychiatry*, **38**, 542–545.

Frank, J. D. (1974). Therapeutic components of psychotherapy: A 25 year progress report of research. *Journal of Nervous and Mental Disease*, **159**, 325–342.

Furman, B. and Ahola, T. (1992). *Solution Talk: Hosting Therapeutic Conversations*. W. W. Norton.

Garcia, E. E. (1990). Somatic interpretation of a transference cure: Freud's treatment of Bruno Walter. *International Review of Psychoanalysis*, **17**, 83–88.

Garfield, S. L. (1978). Research On Client Variables in Psychotherapy. In S. L. Garfield and A. E. Bergin (eds) *Handbook Of Psychotherapy*. Wiley, pp. 191–232.

Garfield, S. L. and Bergins, A. E. (eds) (1971). *Handbook of Psychotherapy and Behavioural Change*.

Gomes-Schwartz, B. (1978). Effective ingredients in psychotherapy: prediction of outcome from process variables. *Journal of Consulting and Clinical Psychology*, **46**, 1023–1035.

Haley, J. (1973) (re-issued 1993). *Uncommon Therapy: The Psychiatric Techniques of Milton H. Erickson, MD*. W. W. Norton.

Haley, J. (1987) (re-issued 1993). *Uncommon Therapy: The Psychiatric Techniques of Milton H. Erickson, MD*. W. W. Norton.

Harland, R. (1987). *Superstructuralism: The Philosophy of Structuralism and Post Structuralism*. Methuen.

Hawkes, D. (1992). *And Never The Twain Shall Meet*. The Ingrebourne Centre Family Therapy Clinic Review, internal document submitted to the Trust's 1992 Mental Health Review.

Hawkes, D. and Marsh, T. I. (1991). *The Ingrebourne Centre Brief Solution Clinic*. Internal document used by the Ingrebourne Centre Therapeutic Community in its Internal Review with the Barking, Havering and Brentwood Trust.

Hawkes, D. and Wilgosh, R. (1991). *Keeping It In The Family*. Internal document published by *Update Magazine*, newsletter of the Barking, Havering and Brentwood Health Authority.

Hawkes, D., Wilgosh, R. and Marsh, T. I. (1992). The what does she know? *Fever Human Systems*, **3**, 67–70.

Hopwood, L. (1992). Introductory Lecture on the Advanced Residency Training. Brief Family Therapy Centre, Milwaukee, USA.

Howard, K. I., Kopta, S. M., Krause, M. S. and Orlinsky, D. E. (1986). The Dose–Effect relationship in psychotherapy. *American Psychologist*, 41, 159–164.

Hunt, D., Hawkes, R., Wilgosh, R. and Adams, P. (1994). *Margins to Mainstream*. Report of Primary Mental Health Care Task Force.

Iseabeart, L. and de Shazer, S. (1997). Submitted for publication at time of press, this reference from internet: solutions.network@skynet.be.

Iveson, D. (1990). Outcome Research What Is It and Who For? MSc Dissertation (Unpublished).

Johnson, L., Lambert, M. (1987). To be published in *Professional Psychology*. Cited on internet: cfranklin@mail.utexas.edu.

Kipling, R. (1991). 'IF' in Rewards and Fairies. Cited in *The Oxford Dictionary of Modern Quotations*. T. Augarde (ed.) Oxford University Press, p. 126.

Kiser, D. (1988). A Follow Up Study Conducted at the Brief Family Therapy Centre. Unpublished manuscript cited in S. de Shazer (1991) *Putting Difference to Work*. Norton, p. 161.

Kiser, D. and Nunnally, E. (1990). The Relationship Between Treatment Length and Goal Achievement in Solution Focused Therapy. Unpublished manuscript cited in S. de Shazer (1991) *Putting Difference to Work*. Norton, p. 171.

Kogan, L. S. (1957). The short-term case in a family agency. Part II results of the study. *Social Case Work*, 38, 396–302.

Koss, M. P. and Butcher, J. N. (1971). Research on Brief Psychotherapy. Chapter 14 in S. L. Garfield and A. E. Bergin (edds) *Handbook of Psychotherapy and Behavioural Change*. Jossey Bass, pp. 627–670.

Kreitman, M. and Dyer, J. A. T. (1980). Suicide in relation to parasuicide. *Mental Education*, pp. 1827–1830.

Lambert, M. J. (1979). Characteristics of patients and their relationship to outcome in Brief Psychotherapy. *Psychiatric Clinics of North America*, 2, 111–124.

Levi, P. (1992). *Dust* from Primo Levi Collected Poems. Faber and Faber, p. 78.

Liberman, B. L., Imber, S. D., Stone, A. R., Hoehn Saric, R. and Frank, J. D. (1974). Mastery: Prescriptive Treatment and Maintenance of Change in Psychotherapy. Cited in J. D. Frank, Therapeutic Components of Psychotherapy. *Journal of Nervous and Mental Disease*, 159, 325–342.

Macdonald, A. J. (1994). Brief Therapy in Adult Psychiatry. *Journal of Family Therapy*, 16, 415–426.

Malan, D. (1968). Psychodynamic changes in untreated neurotic patients I. *British Journal of Psychiatry*, 114, 525–551.

Malan, D. (1975). Psychodynamic changes in untreated neurotic patients II. *Archives of General Psychiatry*, 32, 110–126.

Malan, D. H. (1976). *Toward the Validation of Dynamic Psychotherapy: A Replication*. Plenum.

Malan, D. (1992). *Psychodynamics, Teaching and Outcome in Brief Psychotherapy*. Butterworth-Heinemann.

Mann, J. (1973). *Time Limited Psychotherapy*. Harvard University Press.

Marziali, E., Marmar, C. and Krupnick, J. (1981). Therapeutic alliance scales: development and relationship to psychotherapy outcome. *American Journal of Psychiatry*, 138, 361–364.

McDaniel, S. H., Stiles, W. B. and McGaughey, K. J. (1981). Correlations of male college students verbal response mode use in psychotherapy with measures of psychological disturbance and psychotherapy outcome. *Journal of Consulting and Clinical Psychology*, 49, 571–582.

Minuchin, S. (1974). *Families and Family Therapy*. Harvard University Press.

Molnar, A. and de Shazer, S. (1987). Solution Focused Therapy: toward the identification of therapeutic tasks. *Journal of Marital and Family Therapy*, 13(4), 359–363.

Nash, O. (1983). When you say that smile. From *Candy is Dandy*. Methuen, p. 29.

Noonan, R. J. (1973). A follow up of pretherapy drop outs. *Journal of Community Psychology*, 1, 43–45.

Ockham, W. (1991). Ockhams Razor. From J. O. Urmson and J. Ree (eds) *The Concise Encyclopedia of Western Philosophy and Philosophers*. Routledge, p. 326.

O'Hanlon, W. and Cade, B. (1993). *A Brief Guide to Therapy*.

O'Hanlon, W. and Weiner Davies, M. (1989). *In Search of Solutions: A New Direction in Psychotherapy*. W. W. Norton.

Palazzoli, M. S., Boscolo, L., Checcin, G. and Prata, G. (1978). *Paradox and Counter Paradox*. Aronson.

Pearshall Smith, L. (1991). 'Myself' in Afterthoughts. Cited in *The Oxford Dictionary of Modern Quotations* T. Augarde (ed.) Oxford University Press, p. 42.

Ratner, H., Iveson, C. and George, E. (1990). *Problem to Solution*. Brief Therapy Press.

Salkovskis, P. H., Atha, C., Storer, D. (1990). Cognitive behavioural problem solving in the treatment of patients who repeatedly attempt suicide: a controlled trial. *British Journal of Psychiatry*, 157, p. 871–876.

186 *Solution Focused Therapy*

Sarup, M. (1989). *Post Structuralism and Post Modernism*. University of Georgia Press.
Shakespeare, W. (1991). *Hamlet Prince of Denmark* Act 1 Scene 5. From *The Complete Works of William Shakespeare* Hamlyn, p. 953.
Sifenos, P. E. (1972). *Short Term Psychotherapy and Emotional Crisis*. Harvard University Press.
Sifenos, P. E. (1975). Evaluating the results of short-term anxiety provoking psychotherapy. *Psychotherapy and Psychomatics*, **25**, 217–220.
Silverman, W. H. and Beech, R. P. (1979). Are drop outs really drop outs? *Journal of Community Psychology* 7, 236–242.
Simon, D. (1992). News of the difference. A bulletin board for people who do therapy that makes a difference. *American Solution Focused Newsletter*, **4**, 1.
Sloane, R. B., Staples, F. R., Cristol, A. H. Yorkston, N. J. and Whipple, K. (1975). Short-term analytically oriented psychotherapy versus behaviour therapy. *American Journal of Psychiatry*, **132**, 373–377.
Small, L. (1971). *The Briefer Psychotherapies*. Brunner/Mazel, p. 121.
Smith, M. L., Glass, G. V. and Miller, T. I. (1980). *The Benefits of Psychotherapy*. The Johns Hopkins University Press.
Spoerl, O. H. (1975). Single session psychotherapy. *Diseases of The Nervous System*, **36**, 293–285.
Staples, F. R. and Sloane, R. B. (1970). The relation of speech patterns in psychotherapy to empathic ability, responsiveness to approval and disapproval. *Diseases of The Nervous System*, **31**, 100–104.
Staten, H. (1984). *Wittgenstein and Derrida*. University of Nebraska Press.
Swensen, C. H. (1973). *Introduction to Interpersonal Relations*. Scott Foresman and Co.
Talmon, M. (1990). *Single Session Therapy: Maximising the Effect of the First (and Often Only) Therapeutic Encounter*. Jossey-Bass.
Wallerstein, R. S. (1986). *Forty-two Lives in Treatment: A Study of Psychoanalysis and Psychotherapy*. Guildford.
Wallerstein, R. S. (1989). The psychotherapy research project of the Menninger Foundation: An overview. *Journal of Consulting and Clinical Psychology*, **57** (2), 195–205.
Walter, B. (1947). *Theme and Variations*. Hamish Hamilton.
Watzlawick, P. (1983). *The Situation is Hopeless, But Not Serious: The Pursuit of Unhappiness*. W. W. Norton.
Watzlawick, P. (ed.) (1984). *The Invented Reality: How Do We Know What We Believe We Know?* W. W. Norton.
Watzlawick, P. (1990). *Munchausen's Pigtail or Psychotherapy and Reality*. W. W. Norton.

Watzlawick, P., Weakland, J. and Fisch, R. (1974). *Changes: Principles of Problem Formulation and Problem Resolution.* W. W. Norton.

Weiner Davis, M. (1992). *Divorce Busting.* W. W. Norton.

Weiner Davis, M., de Shazer, S. and Gingerich, W. (1987). Using pre-treatment change to construct a therapeutic solution: An exploratory study. *Journal of Marital and Family Therapy*, 13(3), 359–363.

Wells N. (1981). *Suicide and Deliberate Self Harm.* Office of Health Economics, HMSO.

White, M. and Epston, D. (1990). *Narrative Means to Therapeutic Ends.* W. W. Norton.

Winnicott, D. W. (1982). *Playing and Reality.* Tavistock Publications, p. 84.

Wittgenstein, L. (1958). *Philosophical Investigations.* Macmillan.

'Wittgenstein' (film) (1993). Connoisseur Films distributed by DISC Ref CR 122.

Yallom, I. D. (1931). *Theory and Practice of Group Psychotherapy.* Basic Books.

Index